Awakening
Past Lives

Awakening Past Lives

A Step-by-Step Guide to Self-Exploration

John Z. Amoroso, PhD

4th Dimension Press • Virginia Beach • Virginia

4th Dimension Press is an Imprint of A.R.E. Press

4th Dimension Press
215 67th Street
Virginia Beach, VA 23451–2061

ISBN 13: 978-0-87604-685-2

Cover design by Christine Fulcher

Table of Contents

Section Three: Exploring Your Biographical Life—
An Introspective Process

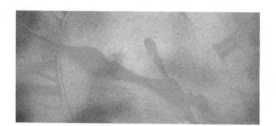

Introduction

Mary's life had been challenging for the past two years. She had been in a romantic relationship with a man who was emotionally not present. He would consistently pull her into the relationship and then find some reason to push her away. In many respects it had been similar to her fifteen-year marriage. That had ended three years ago when she found out that her husband had been carrying on a series of affairs with other women. She came out of these experiences disillusioned and damaged. Her sense of self-esteem and confidence had once again been compromised. In addition, the dynamics in her marriage and this recent relationship had dramatically interfered with what she was realizing as a passion and a new direction in her life. For years she had thought about pursuing a career in nursing, especially now that her children were living out on their own.

After two years of psychotherapy with a reputable therapist, Mary was beginning to realize a pattern that was clearly reflected in these last two romantic relationships. The issue of betrayal and the experiences of being emotionally abandoned and criticized were familiar to her. Her father had been a critical and overbearing character in her life. Her mother, in the face of her father's hostility, became submissive. When Mary was eight years old, her family changed dramatically. Her mother died of cancer, and her father became even more emotionally unavailable. The two years of therapy had uncovered these repeating dynamics in the experiences of her relationships, but her life was not changing. Mary continued to struggle with depression and a sense of hopelessness.

Not long after the breakup of this last relationship, Mary heard about my work in past-life regression therapy on a local radio program. During the first three regression sessions, she uncovered past-life experiences that perfectly corresponded to what had been going on in her life recently. She went to a life where she was the chief of a Native American tribe in which she had been betrayed and persecuted by rival factions. In another life she was the mother of three small children. She had left them alone to find food during a blizzard only to return to find them frozen to death. The guilt of having abandoned her family stayed with her until her death in that life. There were several other past lives during which she was either abandoned or the one who abandoned. Mary's discovery of this abandonment theme in prior lives was the key to her recovery. Her regression work uncovered the roots of this negative theme in her current life. In the course of awakening each of these traumatic episodes in past lives, she gained deeper insight about these negative karmic themes—the abandoned/abandoner. And by reprocessing these traumatic experiences in those lives in a positive way, she was able to "finish that unfinished business" of the past. She could then reach a state of self-forgiveness and forgiveness of her perpetrators. Mary started to feel the depression and hopelessness lift.

Mary was also surprised to discover several lifetimes where she was a caregiver and healer. In these regression sessions we focused on the positive fulfilling feelings and experiences in those lives that formed into positive talents and ways of being. These positive past-life karmic patterns had been carried into this life and formed into a sense of soul purpose that she was just beginning to recognize. As a result of her past-life regression experiences, she was able to validate and enliven those positive aspects of herself that formed her sense of soul purpose. By also de-energizing those karmic patterns that had interfered with her relationships and true calling, she had cleared the way for a new life. Mary found herself attracting new relationships that were unburdened by her abandonment theme out of her traumatic karmic past.

It wasn't long before Mary finished nursing school and got a job in a local hospital. Soon after that, she found a romantic relationship unlike any she had ever experienced. Mary is now remarried and happily pursuing her passion for nursing and caregiving.

Mary's story is a perfect example of how past-life regression works. It explains how exploring and processing past-life experiences can give one a deeper insight into the dynamics of both positive and negative themes/complexes that are carried into one's life. It was through this approach that Mary was able to finally release herself from these persistent dysfunctional themes and to successfully refocus on and energize the positive. Although she started out skeptical of the idea of reincarnation, she was still able to use the principles of karma and the experience of exploring past lives to gain insight and to change her life for the better.

The objective of this book is to provide you with the tools to start the process of awakening past lives on the path of healing and growth. Through the use of discussion, self-reflection, journaling, and Integrated Imagery exercises found throughout this book, you will have the opportunity to:

- Explore and de-energize the negative karmic themes from other times.
- Uncover and accentuate the positive karmic themes.
- Discover and enliven your unique sense of soul purpose.

This excursion through past lives and your biographical experiences may simply help you to validate what you already know about yourself. But don't be surprised if you discover new insights that will contribute to your mission of healing and growth.

The Philosophy of Reincarnation

Reincarnation thinking is a belief grounded in the idea that we have lived before and that we will live again. It explains that our current life personalities, patterns of behavior, skills, interests, sensitivities, difficulties, and even physical conditions tend to have their roots in past lives. It espouses that the purpose of life is soul growth which requires the resolution of negative disruptive patterns and the enabling of the positive enlivening aspects of one's soul.

Reincarnation thinking also infers that we come into a life with a specific soul purpose or life mission. Based on our personal karmic or past-life history, it can involve a vocation or avocation, an interest, or simply a way of being in the world. In any case, it is personal and unique for each of us, and it encompasses those positive themes or aspects of ourselves. It is the negative disruptive themes from past lives (the unfinished business) that can block or disrupt the ability to realize one's soul purpose. Mary was able to pursue her new career as a nurse only after she released herself from those patterns of behavior and relationships that stifled her self-confidence. Consequently, she began to attract healthy intimate relationships into her life.

There is no better example of the workings of karma and past-life influences than the intuited psychic readings of Edgar Cayce. The vast majority of these readings focused on medical ailments and recommended treatments for those conditions. However, in nearly two thousand of the more than fourteen thousand readings, Cayce specifically referred to past-life experiences as the root of these ailments and the implications of soul purpose. In Chapters One and Two we'll talk more about those readings, the philosophy of reincarnation, and the history of past-life regression.

As indicated in the Cayce readings and by reincarnation thinking in general, we can think of ourselves as spiritual beings on an evolutionary path of growth and learning that spans many lifetimes. The process of soul growth can be compared to progressing through high school, college, and graduate school with each life corresponding to a different course of study. Mary's mission in this life is to deal with the theme of abandonment and to learn to accentuate her positive themes on the way to realizing her full potential and soul purpose. If she were to fail to learn these lessons, she would have another opportunity to review this same experience in a subsequent lifetime—she could retake the course, so to speak. This is exactly what we all face in life: to complete the unfinished business of the past and to continue the positive experiences of former lives. Therefore, as the Cayce readings so clearly indicate, we go on incarnating until there is no longer a need—until we graduate to higher consciousness. For this reason we'll be using the metaphysical system defined in the readings as an important set of guidelines for the regression exercises in this book.

The History of Reincarnation Thinking

Reincarnation thinking certainly was a dominant principle in the Cayce readings, but this philosophy of rebirth has a much deeper history. It has been a central theme not only in the Eastern religious traditions, such as Buddhism and Hinduism, but also in the ancient philosophies dating back to the Greeks as well as most of the primitive religions. The idea of rebirth is also seen throughout the Aboriginal cultures, the Inuit people, most African tribes, and the Native American religions. Virtually all of the esoteric spiritual philosophies from Theosophy and Anthroposophy to the intuited readings of Edgar Cayce and most other psychics and channels attest to the principles of rebirth, karma, and soul development. Theological scholars have also discovered evidence of reincarnation philosophy in the mystical sects of our Western religions of Judaism, Christianity, and Islam. It is estimated that more than half of all the people who have ever lived have believed in reincarnation.

In our modern times, a 1969 Gallup Poll in ten western countries—including the US—indicated that from 18 to 26 percent of the people believe in reincarnation with the US population at 20 percent. Other polls more than twelve years later showed that these numbers had grown to 23 percent in the US with 67 percent of the population believing in life after death. Amazingly, 78 percent of Brazilians were found to believe in reincarnation in similar polls. By 2005 polls stated that three out of four Americans held some belief in the paranormal including astrology, clairvoyance, and reincarnation.

Past-Life Regression Therapy

Considering this increase in the belief in past lives, it is not surprising that past–life regression therapy has gained validity as an effective psychotherapeutic technique in the last thirty years (especially when looking at the spiritual or transpersonal dimensions of life). An interesting point is that this idea of regressing to past lives for healing and growth has been researched and used as a therapeutic technique as far back as the late 1800s. Past–life regression therapy has essentially grown up alongside of modern psychology and psychotherapy. More psychotherapists and counselors than ever are learning the techniques of regression therapy. Articles and books continue to be published confirming the effectiveness of this approach.

My interest in reincarnation and past–life regression was sparked in my late thirties when I read *There Is a River* by Thomas Sugrue, talking about the life and intuited readings of Edgar Cayce. Over the next several years I became absorbed with the history of reincarnation thinking, karmic influence, and the use of past–life regression as a therapeutic technique. By the late 1980s I was enrolled in a PhD program in clinical psychology where I was able to continue my research in past–life regression therapy while studying the established principles and methods in modern psychology and psychotherapy.

I had discovered a new direction in my life and work which resonated with my soul purpose. At this time Dr. Harmon Bro became one of the most significant influences in my life. He was a gifted scholar, author, and spiritual mentor who had known Edgar Cayce during the last years of Cayce's life. Harmon encouraged and mentored me through this midlife transition that would become my life's work. While completing my doctoral studies, I was able to study Ericksonian hypnosis, Gestalt therapy, psychodrama, and Core Energetic therapy. In addition, I was also fortunate to learn the approach and techniques of Dr. Morris Netherton and to work with Dr. Roger Woolger—both major contributors to the field of past–life regression therapy.

I have used this approach of past–life regression for more than twenty years in my own psychotherapy practice. I am convinced of its effectiveness. In the course of conducting thousands of regression sessions, I have developed an approach that I call Integrated Imagery. Through the use of hypnosis and guided imagery in combination with current psychotherapeutic methods, this is an experiential process that enables clients to regress to prior times and altered states of consciousness in order to uncover and deal with the details of the unfinished business that are the antecedents of negative themes (or complexes) that persist in their lives. At the same time, what is unique about this method is that it leads them to examine, enliven, and refocus on the positive themes that also form in their prior-life experiences. This is very much a process of accentuating the positive and de-energizing the negative while awakening insights regarding one's unique sense of soul purpose.

Integrated Imagery is also different from most other approaches in that during the course of the regression process, the subject is guided to awaken not only past lives but between-life states, before-life states, and the nine-month perinatal experiences between conception and birth. The experiences and insights from these other dimensions or from what I call the "energetic chains of experience" are then integrated into the biographical life.

In past lives we uncover the traumatic and enlivening experiences that formed and reinforced the positive and negative karmic patterns. In the between-life state the client is able to gain insights regarding the relevance of those experiences to his/her biographical life. The before-life state provides the opportunity to observe the soul-level decision process regarding the lesson plan for the forthcoming life while the perinatal experience reveals the early manifestations of the karmic past-life patterns in this life. The result of this holistic, integrated process is that the subject is able to uncover and to deepen self-understanding in the context of soul purpose and spiritual development.

Another distinguishing feature of Integrated Imagery is that it makes use of and defines a new psychological model for understanding human behavior—complex psychology. This model is an expansion of Carl Jung's idea of complexes, and it provides a much clearer insight as to how and why past-life experiences affect our current lives.

As part of my work with clients in counseling, therapy, and group sessions, I developed an extensive set of exercises based on the techniques in Integrated Imagery so that they might continue their personal journey of self-discovery between sessions and after finishing formal therapy. These are the exercises you will use throughout the rest of this book. They start with a careful examination of your biographical life experiences before moving on to the regression exercises in the last section.

How to Use This Book

In the first section, I will introduce the ancient roots of reincarnation thinking and the principles of karma that provide some insight as to how and why past-life regression or Integrated Imagery can be so effective. I'll also talk about the philosophy of past-life influence and soul purpose as described in the intuitive psychic readings of Edgar Cayce. The metaphysical system in the readings has become an important foundation for the technique of Integrated Imagery. We'll also trace the perhaps surprising history of past-life therapy that grew up alongside of modern psychology and psychotherapy. Finally, to set the stage for your own journey of awakening, I'll present details regarding Integrated Imagery in the process of soul development. This first section will help prepare you for your personal journey of self-discovery.

The second section presents a detailed explanation of the mechanism within the human psyche that forms both the positive and negative themes we all bring into our current life. These positive and negative themes form into complexes that harbor the feelings, images, scripts, physical sensations, and behaviors that we carry into this life. Most important, it gives some insight as to how these karmic themes function and interact with each other. As you proceed through these first two sections, you'll have exercises to start the process. I also encourage you to be aware of how these ideas and examples stimulate insights about your own life.

In Section Three, you'll start your self-exploration process in earnest. The two chapters in this section provide the opportunity to reflect even more directly on the experiences of this life and on the positive, negative, and soul purpose themes that are prominent. Through the use of an autobiographical time line, self-reflection, and journaling, you will start to clarify what you already know about yourself. Moreover the technique of Active Imagination—developed by Carl Jung—will further deepen this process of reflection. To start each Active Imagination session in section three, you'll use the progressive relaxation exercise on Track One of the enclosed CD. This is a recording of my voice guiding you into a state of relaxation and self-reflection.

It is in Section Four that you will have the opportunity to use the tools of Integrated Imagery to carry on your own personal regression and awakening process. In this last section you'll use the guiding sessions on the enclosed CD (Tracks Two through Five) to regress back through past-life, between-life, before-life, and the perinatal experiences on this path of accentuating the positive and de-energizing the negative.

One Important Point to Remember

Throughout this process of exploring your energetic chain of experience, it is not necessary for you to have an absolute belief in reincarnation. These tools and techniques can work whether you are a believer, a skeptic, or a non-believer.

The experience of George is a case in point. It was during the final stages of preparing this book for publication that a prime example of the effectiveness of Integrated Imagery came about.

I was doing a professional training workshop in Integrated Imagery for a group at Atlantic University in Virginia Beach. Atlantic University is a part of the A.R.E. (the Association for Research and Enlightenment—the Edgar Cayce organization) offering master's degree programs in Transpersonal Studies and Practices. I started the fourth and final day of the workshop with a lecture to be followed by a demonstration with one of the participants in the training. During the lecture the receptionist from the A.R.E. came in to announce that a man was here to look into to doing some hypnosis for a problem he was having. We realized he was in the wrong place—or so we thought. Apparently, he was exploring the idea of doing a hypnosis session with a hypnotherapist based at the A.R.E. clinic next door to the conference center. I told the receptionist to ask him to come back within the hour to talk about his problem. At that point we were all curious about the synchronicity of this occurrence.

He did come back and we spent a little time talking about his problem. George was a pilot flying F/A-18 fighter jets based at the Naval Air Station in Norfolk. His problem was that he had been experiencing over the last several years severe bouts of nausea during routine training flights. It seems that for no reason—with no turbulence—he would start to vomit for up to two hours at a time while in flight. The medics couldn't explain these episodes, and George was concerned that he would be grounded unless he got a handle on the problem. To compound the situation, he was scheduled to be shipped out with the fleet within the next two days.

In the process of talking about his problem, I explained that I did regression work through hypnosis and that a session might address such an issue. George agreed to discuss the problem in front of the group and to go through a regression to explore the real problem at hand. As we discussed the bouts of vomiting in front of the training group, I asked him if he believed in reincarnation. To my surprise he said, "No, not at all." Then I asked if he had ever heard of Edgar Cayce. It was even more surprising when he answered "no" again. In spite of his disbelief, he agreed to do the past–life regression session.

I started the regression with the normal progressive relaxation exercise and eventually with the suggestion that he allow himself to explore the reasons for these episodes of vomiting that interfered with his flights. He almost immediately went back to a life during the Second World War. In that life he was a gunner on an American bomber flying missions over Germany. During one mission the plane was damaged by a German fighter plane and the bomber safely landed with all crew members aboard. George's past-life character felt pangs of guilt that he had not managed to shoot down the German plane. I then suggested that he move to the moments leading up to his death in that life. At that point he was on another bombing mission where he again missed a shot at an attacking German plane. This time the bomber was severely damaged, and the crew was instructed to bail out over Germany. As George's character bailed out, he was filled with fear and guilt that he had missed the shot. He then realized that his parachute wouldn't open. As he plummeted to the ground and to his death, the severe feeling of nausea came over him and all he could think about were his mother and his girlfriend who he would never see again. That life ended with the karmic imprint of fear, loss, and guilt that formed into a complex and that manifested in this life in a purely physical reaction through his vomiting attacks.

To end the session I had him go back into the dying experience and reprocess the event by releasing the feelings that surrounded that traumatic event. In one pass I had him go back into the past–life experience and imagine that his parachute did open and that he and his crew members survived. In another pass, I guided him through an experience where he did shoot down the German fighter plane, and the bomber returned safely to home base. We then revisited the between–life state where George was able to further discharge the guilt and fear that he had carried with him on a soul level.

George was clearly shocked by his regression experience, but he did report a sense of peace that came over him during the process of integration. What was most interesting was that he reported he had purposely stayed clear of having a girlfriend while he was in the service. Unfortunately, I had no opportunity to do any follow–up sessions with George because he was scheduled to ship out with the fleet. With a client in therapy, I would have done several more sessions to be sure of the resolution of the problem at hand. It will usually take more than one regression to completely clear a karmic complex. I consequently had no contact with George for some time. It was six months later that I accidently found his email address in my files. I was immediately moved to contact him to ask how he was doing. Within fifteen minutes he sent back the following message:

John,
Well, flying has been great for the military . . . haven't had one problem with nausea since the session and am soon to be doing
....
Thanks for all your help . . .
George

Fortunately, that single regression session was enough to relieve George of the karmic pattern that he carried into this life. By awakening the past-life trauma surrounding that experience, we were able to de-energize the complex that had manifested as a physical reaction. In the case of George, we have a prime example of the effectiveness of Integrated Imagery and the impact that past-life experiences can have on our current lives, regardless of the subject's beliefs. George was clearly a non-believer, and it still worked. It appears that George is free of this pattern that had been such a problem in his career. Hopefully, George can go on from here and eventually find himself a girlfriend. At the very least, we can be certain that we have a talented, committed, and healthy pilot in service to our country.

An Exercise to Start Your Awakening Process

An important first step in this process of awakening is to prepare your *autobiographical time line*. Take whatever time you need to start to identify the stages, phases, and incidents in your life history that are the most obvious and significant. You'll use the time line throughout the rest of the exercises to follow.

Prepare for the Exercise:
- Find a quiet and comfortable place where you can relax and reflect on your life—a place where you will not be disturbed.
- Have 8 1/2" x 11" sheets of paper (one for each decade of your life), a notebook or journal, pens/pencils, crayons, and a ruler with you.
- Draw a line across the bottom of each of the 8 1/2" x 11" sheets of paper (turned horizontally) to represent ten years of your life. You can notate each year on the line with a mark. Do a separate sheet for each ten-year period.

Start the Exercise:
As you proceed with this exercise, it's best to focus on one ten-year period at a time. Take as much time as you need to reflect on your life and the experiences in that period before going on to the next period.
- Start by relaxing with a few deep breaths and letting go of any ten-

sion in your body. Take as much time as you need to relax into a quiet, safe reflective feeling.

- As you reflect and uncover memories, draw shorter horizontal lines to represent the significant periods in your life—for example, time spent in different levels of schooling; periods of involvement in hobbies, interests, and extra-curricular activities; periods of time when you lived in a specific location; times working at different jobs, and times when you were involved in significant relationships. These lines represent significant phases of your life.
- On these shorter time lines, indicate specific events that represent transition points (when your life changed) at the beginning, middle, or end of those significant phases. These could involve people you met, opportunities that came to you, insights you had, or decisions you made.
- As you reflect, remember specific incidents that occur to you that are significant.
- Remember how you felt, the people involved, what you were thinking as well as what was happening at the time.

For now, make any notations on your time line and in your journal regarding any ideas or insights that come to you. In the following exercises you'll be expanding on these notations and insights.

As you read through the chapters in Section One, be aware of any additional images or insights that come to you regarding the history of reincarnation thinking, karmic philosophy, or the technique of past-life regression and Integrated Imagery. Be sure to come back to your time line and record those insights, whether they make sense at the time or not.

Remember: with the exercises throughout this book, the more you practice, the easier it will be for you to access these memories and insights.

Finally, relax, take a soothing breath, and enjoy your journey of awakening past lives on the path of self-exploration.

Section One:
Reincarnation Thinking in Perspective

In this section, we'll start this journey of awakening and self-discovery with a short excursion through the history of reincarnation thinking and past-life regression and then deal with a definition of the laws of karma that seem to dictate the implications of our past lives. As you'll see, in one form or another, the idea of past lives and rebirth has been a dominant thought throughout recorded time. To put these ideas into a modern perspective we'll also look in some detail at the metaphysical system as explained in the intuited psychic readings of Edgar Cayce—the Sleeping Prophet of our times. Finally, we'll define the technique of Integrated Imagery that you'll be using in your personal journey of self-exploration.

Chapter 1

The History of Reincarnation Thinking and Past-Life Regression

As you start this journey of self-discovery, it will be helpful to understand the extensive history of reincarnation thinking throughout the ages as well as the modern history of past-life regression therapy. As we'll see, the philosophy of reincarnation comes in many versions. The common thread in all of these versions, however, is the idea that we have lived before and we will probably live again in some process of soul growth. In one form or another we carry themes and issues from life to life in the process. It is this common thread that is the guiding principle in the technique of past-life regression therapy.

The Eastern Religious Traditions

When most of us think of the process of rebirth and soul growth, we naturally turn to the Eastern spiritual philosophies. There are very clearly written references to reincarnation going back to the earliest scriptures of the Hindu religion. Although Hindu scholars have debated reincarnation, there are indications of this belief system as far back as the *Rig Veda* written around 1500 BC. Other classic Hindu scriptures, especially the Upanishads (600 BC), and the Bhagavad Gita and Mahabharata written centuries later, even more directly emphasize the philosophy of reincarnation and karmic process.

Although there are some variations regarding the workings of reincarnation within Hinduism, the general concept holds that human souls have emanated from a Supreme Being. Through many incarnations those souls forgot their divine origin or true spiritual nature. It is in the process of subsequent incarnations that souls may begin to realize their true nature as emanations of that Supreme presence. We have the opportunity to return home. As the philosophy dictates, man must essentially disengage from the ego attachments of the material life and become open to his already present spiritual essence while in the material plan. In this process of growth man must learn through experience and free will to release himself from the imperfections and distractions of the material life.

It was in the sixth century BC that the Buddhist religion started in India as a reaction to the rigid social and moral code of Hinduism. Over the years Buddhism spread throughout Asia taking on different forms based on the local culture. The common thread throughout the various forms of Buddhism—and with Hinduism itself—is the idea of rebirth and the workings of karma. Buddhism espouses the repetition of lives until *moksha* or the liberation of the soul from material existence—in Buddhist terms enlightenment. In spite of minor differences in the process of karma or the rules dictating which lessons and patterns are carried forward from one life to another, the major distinction from Hindu philosophy has to do with the personal nature of the soul. In Buddhism the soul lacks a permanent sense of self whereas Hinduism maintains the idea that the soul itself is evolving through the many incarnations. In either case the principle of soul growth is present.

The Mahayana form of Buddhism in the north of Asia presents another variance and principle worth noting. It maintains that Boddhisattvas who have achieved nirvana or enlightenment may continue to incarnate as helpers out of compassion for the still suffering humanity. This form clearly emphasizes not only the idea of growth but also that of service to humanity. The concept of service to humanity which we'll see is very much the essence of living one's soul purpose.

Around the time of the emergence of Buddhism in India, another religion would spring up—Jainism. With a much smaller following Jainism would hold to the same tenets of rebirth and soul development but with a slightly different take on how past–life experiences carried forward. Jainists believe that karma is solely dependent on the consequences of an act in a past life with little to do with the intent of that act. In this way, for example, unintentionally causing death has the same results and future–life consequences as premeditated murder. Jainists, therefore, tend to be more conscientious about how they consciously and unconsciously engage in life with an intense focus on unremitting service to others.

The Primitive and Preliterate Spiritual Philosophies

It's probably safe to say that most Westerners believe that reincarnation philosophy is the province of Eastern religious traditions. As stated by scholar and past–life researcher Hans TenDam in *Exploring Reincarnation*, a book published in 1987,

> "The general assumption that reincarnation is a typically Indian idea is as persistent as it is wrong. Ideas about reincarnation are found in diverse cultures all over the world. . . . Anthropologically, belief in reincarnation is better conceived as an original category which has arisen independently in separate cultures."[1]

So Eastern religions do not have a corner on reincarnation thinking after all. In fact, most of the preliterate or primitive religions as far back as the Stone Age also consider the idea of preexistence of the soul and rebirth.

In Africa reincarnation is prominent in almost one hundred native

---

[1]Hans TenDam, *Exploring Reincarnation* (London: Arkana Press, 1987), 29.

tribes. The Zulu tribes, for example, maintain sophisticated beliefs including the idea that gradual perfection is the result of many incarnations until return to the material life is no longer necessary. In West Africa, where the belief is the strongest, reincarnation is viewed as good for a soul, and people prefer to come back into the same family.

Among the primitive aboriginal tribes in Australia, historians have confirmed that reincarnation was a universal belief that spread throughout the Pacific Islands. Again, many of the details of the process of rebirth vary among these Asian cultures, but the common thread is that of recycling and soul growth.

In the America's from the ancient Mayans, the Incas, and the primitive tribes throughout South America up to the native tribes of Canada and Alaska, reincarnation philosophy was a prominent belief.

Among the Native American tribes the philosophy and rituals around the return of the spirit to another body was especially deep-rooted and widespread, especially in the northeast. Throughout North America from the tribes of the Pueblos, Hopi, Dakotas, and Lakotas to the Iroquois and Lenape of Delaware, reincarnation was thought of as a positive aspect of their spiritual nature.

The Early European History

Considering the history of these ancient cultures, it should not be surprising that reincarnation thinking was prominent among the early European cultures. The Celts in northern Europe held a belief unusually similar to Eastern philosophies. They maintained that after many lifetimes one's soul would achieve a "white heaven" in the presence of God. Even those who lived badly had the opportunity to achieve this divine existence provided they corrected the misdeeds of the past. As in the Buddhist concept of the Boddhisattva, those who have achieved purification could come back to help others until everyone realized the white heaven. Throughout ancient Europe from the Danes, Norse, Finns, and Icelanders in the north down to the Bretons, Saxons, and Lombards in Italy, all demonstrated various versions of rebirth and soul growth. We can surmise, even without the benefit of past-life regression therapy, how these beliefs affected the way the people in these cultures lived their lives.

As far back as the early Greeks in the sixth century BC, scholars have confirmed the belief in transmigration of souls and reincarnation thinking. Herodotus, a Greek historian in the fifth century BC, even inferred that these beliefs dated back to the Egyptians. Throughout Greek mythology we see symbols and references to death, rebirth, and purification of the soul. The Greek mathematician and philosopher Pythagoras (500 BC) taught reincarnation thinking and even claimed to have remembered his own prior lifetimes. Plato very clearly expressed elaborate theories of rebirth and karmic laws—closely corresponding to Eastern beliefs—in his many written works. Even Aristotle around 384 BC described reincarnation in his early works. What is apparent throughout Greek history is that these beliefs remained in the domain of the philosophers and intellectuals of the time and were isolated from the beliefs of the general population.

As we'll see, the idea of reincarnation was completely eliminated from Christian philosophy in Europe by the fifth century AD. Even so, the Renaissance brought a resurgence of this idea with the revisiting of Plato's works known as Neoplatonism. These ideas from the 1400s would manage to stay alive at least among philosophers, writers, artists, and theologians right into the current times.

Judaism, Christianity, and Islam

With such a pervasive history in Eastern and ancient traditions, how is it that reincarnation thinking does not appear in our modern Western religions? There is an explanation. Especially within the last fifty years, it has become clear that these principles of preexistence and rebirth were a part of the early teachings and especially the mystical sects of all three of our Western religious traditions.

In the early days of Judaism and around the time of Jesus, there were three major schools of Jewish philosophy. Of these, only the Sadducees believed in the death of the soul at the time of physical death. The Essenes, thought to be responsible for the education of Jesus, believed in the preexistence of the soul with indications in scholarly writings of a belief in rebirth. The Pharisees believed even more firmly in the notion of reincarnation up until the ninth century.

The Kabbalistic movement within Judaism came into prominence in the Middle Ages. This mystical sect in Judaism held very strong and distinctive beliefs which clearly advocate the purification of the soul through reincarnation. Scholars have even managed to trace the earliest roots of the Kabbalistic movement back to Aryan sources or the pre-Hindu influence in the Indus Valley of India.

In the earlier days of this sect, Kabbalism was considered the domain of the advanced practitioner of Judaism. It was in the sixteenth century that it experienced resurgence among the common Jew during the Spanish Inquisition with the expulsion of the Jews from Spain. Since then the presence of reincarnation thinking all but disappeared among the general Jewish community except for one sect—the Hasidic Jews. This small Jewish sect formed during the eighteenth century in Poland. To this day, according to the *Universal Jewish Encyclopedia*, this group advocates preexistence of the soul and rebirth along with the principles of karma similar to the Eastern beliefs.

Reincarnation and Christianity

When it comes to reincarnation philosophy in Christianity, there is a more interesting story to tell. Reincarnationists for years have pointed to many references in the New Testament regarding preexistence of the soul, rebirth, and the concept of soul development and causality that constitute reincarnation thinking. Theological scholars have also identified these ideas in the writings of the early church fathers of the first, second, and third centuries as they debated the teachings of Jesus. It was the discovery of the Gnostic Gospels in Nag Hammadi in 1945 that confirmed the early presence of reincarnation thinking in Christian history. The writings of this early Gnostic sect were filled with references to reincarnation and the process of soul growth. The reason why this philosophy did not survive in modern Christianity is apparent when we look at the early evolution of the religion in the context of the Roman Empire.

Origen, the third century religious scholar of Greek heritage, is considered the most notable and influential of all theologians of the ancient church. In several surviving works and many commentaries by other church fathers, Origen put forth the idea of the preexistence of the soul and a version of reincarnation philosophy. Origen died in 254 and by 312 AD Emperor Constantine had converted the Roman Empire to Christianity. Even then, the principles of reincarnation and the ideas of Origen were still controversial within the church teachings. Origen's ideas were one of many factors causing discord among the various Christian factions within the Empire. It was in 553 at the Council of Constantinople that Emperor Justinian put an end to the controversy of reincarnation by condemning the teachings of Origen. Many theological scholars consider this declaration a turning point in the consideration of reincarnation in Christian philosophy. With this move by Justinian, those factions within the church who maintained the belief in reincarnation were forced underground. Most dominant among those early sects was the Gnostic movement. It was believed, in fact, that they were the direct descendants of those who were privy to the secret teachings of Jesus. These special teachings are alluded to in Mark 4:11 when Jesus says, "Unto you it is given to know the mystery of the Kingdom of God; but unto them that are without all those things are done in parables."

Aside from reincarnation, the Gnostics held many beliefs and practices which are contradictory to current Christian doctrine. Suffice it to say, these principles and practices including the concept of equality of the sexes and the idea that spiritual practice was a personal affair requiring only a direct connection between the follower and God were enough to threaten the church hierarchy and the control it wielded over its followers. These teachings did survive, however, in several Gnostic sects including the Cathars, the Albigensians, and the Knights Templar through the Middle Ages. And they also realized a modest resurgence during the Neoplatonic movement in Renaissance Italy. But it wasn't until the discovery of the Gnostic Gospels in 1945 that the significance of reincarnation thinking in Christianity was confirmed.

Reincarnation in the Religion of Islam

The religion of Islam has a much less complex history regarding the belief in reincarnation. Although there are no direct references to reincarnation in the Koran, some scholars have speculated that Mohammed, as did Jesus, taught this philosophy to advanced followers. It is, however, the mystical sect of the Sufis that has a strong belief in rebirth and soul growth. This teaching associates rebirth with conscious evolution. It is Jalal Rumi (1207–1273), one of Persia's great mystical poets, who wrote about the advancement of our souls from the lowest material forms to a point of unity with each other and God as in the beginning.

In Conclusion

From this short excursion through history we can see why many scholars and historians might consider reincarnation as such a pervasive belief. We can see why Hans TenDam would claim that "reincarnation thinking has been embraced for more than half the time of recorded history by more than half the population."[2] Throughout history every continent on the globe has housed great cultures that believed in reincarnation in one form or another.

Of course there are different versions of the belief regarding the number of incarnations, what carries forward, the nature of lessons, the intermission time between lives, whether or not we have a choice, and the family affiliations we come into. What is consistent throughout the history of reincarnation thinking is the principle that rebirth is about the evolution of the soul.

Reincarnation makes so much more sense of life than our Western religious traditions teach. For one, we have more than one chance to achieve a good life. We have free will to make conscious choices about how to live. We carry both positive and negative imprints or themes that make up our lesson plan for a given life. Life is purposeful in the process of healing and growth. And finally, reincarnation explains the inequities of life—we are, in fact, not all born equal. We carry into this life themes and complexes from the past that are unique to each of us. These ideas and principles are clearly reflected in the work of Edgar Cayce—a modern day prophet.

---

[2]Hans TenDam, *Exploring Reincarnation* (London: Arkana Press, 1987), 51.

The Life of Edgar Cayce

Edgar Cayce was a medical intuitive and spiritual philosopher who came to national attention in the early part of the twentieth century as a result of his medical readings. These readings conducted through a self-induced trance state with a guide present constitute the most extensive collection of psychic readings in the Western world. Over the course of 14,306 psychic transmissions, Cayce focused on the diagnosis of physical, mental, and emotional disorders and the prescription of a combination of homeopathy, osteopathy, herbology, home-spun medicine, and spiritual remedies. The advice provided proved to be incredibly successful in relieving symptoms and in healing—even those in some cases considered hopeless. Through the years Cayce scholars have studied the readings in an attempt to determine the actual effectiveness of these diagnoses and prescriptions. The general consensus is that his accuracy rate is estimated in excess of 80 percent.

Edgar Cayce was born to a poor Kentucky farming family in 1877. He spent the better part of his childhood focused as much on Bible studies as on his schoolwork. Before the age of twenty-one he had only strange inklings of his psychic abilities. It was at twenty-one in 1901 that Cayce's skill became apparent. While working as a salesman, he developed a persistent laryngitis. With no relief for almost a year, he allowed himself to be hypnotized by Al C. Layne, a local practitioner of hypnosis. While Cayce was in a trance state, Layne suggested that he diagnose his affliction and suggest a remedy. The result of the hypnosis session was extraordinary. His laryngitis was cured. It was shortly thereafter that Layne asked for a reading and remedy for his own affliction with the same results. Those first medical readings started Edgar Cayce on the path of a modern-day mystic.

During his bout with laryngitis, Cayce changed his work out of necessity to become a professional photographer to support his wife Gertrude and their growing family. It wasn't long, however, before he was doing medical readings on a full-time basis. As the word spread, requests for these healing insights started to pour in from around the country. With only the name of the individual, who was usually hundreds of miles away, Cayce would start his reading by self-inducing a trance and then stating, "Yes, we have the body here." Eventually the readings drew the attention of medical professionals interested in the validity and effectiveness of the medial advice coming out of the readings. Cayce consistently impressed these detractors and supporters alike with the impact of the healing readings.

In 1923 Cayce agreed to do a reading conducted by Arthur Lammers. Lammers, who was a businessman as well as a student of metaphysics and astrology, asked specific questions regarding his past-life history. This was the first of more than nineteen hundred "life readings" that indicated the karmic past-life background of the subject's ailments and started to address the idea of soul purpose. Prior to that first life reading, no mention was made of reincarnation, soul purpose, or the spiritual aspects of the subject's life. From that point on, a complete metaphysical system started to emerge. We'll talk about that system in more detail in the next chapter. Suffice it to say, the principles described in the readings perfectly correlate to the ideas we talked about in the long history of reincarnation thinking.

Around the same time, Cayce's personal readings started to indicate the need to move to the seaside resort of Virginia Beach. Along with this suggestion was the idea to form an organization to house the readings and undertake research with an adjacent hospital to administer the recommended remedies. It was also around this time that several supporters and investors gathered to encourage the move. By 1925 the Cayce family had relocated to Virginia Beach, and the first formal organization and hospital were formed. After several years of financial difficulty, a second organization—the Association for Research and Enlightenment—was chartered along with the hospital. Then Atlantic University was organized in 1930 to provide the general public the opportunity to study the spiritual philosophy that was the foundation of the readings. Both the A.R.E. and Atlantic University evolved over the next fifty years under the direction of Cayce's son Hugh Lynn and his grandson Charles Thomas Cayce. To this day the A.R.E. and Atlantic University flourish with the mission of preserving the Cayce legacy, enabling ongoing research and service to humanity.

Edgar Cayce died in 1945 after spending more than forty-four years counseling people through the readings. The remedies he prescribed during his readings proved to be very effective in healing the ailments of his subjects. His intuitive insights about past lives, karma, and soul purpose served to support their healing process and soul growth by explaining the influence of their prior incarnations on their biographical lives.

For more than a century, however, a body of work was developing that would give everyone the opportunity to make use of past-life insight in personal journeys of healing, self-discovery, and soul growth.

The History of Past-Life Regression

It may be surprising to know that the research and development of past-life regression as a psychotherapeutic technique grew up side-by-side with the field of modern psychology.

The beginning of modern psychology goes back to the work of Wilhelm Wundt in 1879 in Leipzig, Germany. His psychological model, which viewed human behavior from the standpoint of cause and effect, evolved to this day into what is behavioral psychology. By the late 1900s, Sigmund Freud was on the scene in Vienna. His psychoanalytic movement refocused the study of human behavior and psychotherapy on the idea that the unconscious mind harbored experiences and behavioral reactions from the past that affected current behavior. It took almost sixty years before the work of Abraham Maslow, Carl Rogers, and Rollo May would gain prominence in the humanistic schools of psychology. Fundamental to this approach is the idea of the inescapable uniqueness of individual human consciousness, the individual as a unified whole, and the drive to continually evolve toward self-actualization. The fourth movement in modern psychology—transpersonal psychology—came to prominence shortly thereafter embracing the principles out of the other three movements while emphasizing the spiritual aspects of humanity. Those are the spiritual aspects that focus on the idea of soul growth while evolving to reunite with the Divine.

The Early Days of Past-Life Regression Therapy

Even prior to the development of modern psychology, there were recorded incidences of past–life recollections and the healing effect of those experiences. It wasn't until 1911, however, that a formal academic publication of past–life recall would appear. In *Les Vies successives*, Albert de Rochas wrote of his ten years of research on the use of past–life regression as a psychotherapeutic technique. He found that clients, through hypnosis, would report not only past–life experiences but recollections of in utero and birth experiences whether they believed in reincarnation or not. Carrying on the work of de Rochas was John Bjorkhem of Sweden and Dr. Alexander Cannon of England. During the first half of the 1900s, Cannon personally recorded over fourteen hundred regression sessions while documenting the clinical benefits of his approach.

Influenced by these early researchers and by Cayce, a Colorado businessman named Morey Bernstein started to experiment with hypnosis and past–life regression in 1952 with a Pueblo housewife—Virginia Tighe. In the regression experiences that followed she went back to the life of Bridey Murphy in County Cork Ireland in the nineteenth century. Through a series of sessions it was revealed that Bridey Murphy was born in 1798 to a Protestant barrister and his wife. Before her death in 1864, she married a Catholic barrister and lived in Belfast. When the book *The Search for Bridey Murphy* was published in 1956, it became an instant bestseller stimulating controversy, investigations, and speculation that would last for years. In spite of the verified information that came out of the regressions regarding people, places, and circumstances, debunkers managed to shed enough doubt on the credibility of the story that it remains unresolved to this day. In any case, the Bridey Murphy incident gained international attention and purportedly stimulated a great deal of attention regarding the implications of past–life regression among the general public as well as the professional psychological community.

It was around the same time of Morey Bernstein's experiments with past–life regression that a young physician started to explore past–life regression as a therapeutic technique. Of all of the early contemporary investigators in the field of past–life therapy, Dr. Denys Kelsey has been considered by many to be a pioneer in the field. Kelsey first started to use hypnosis as a medical resident in 1948 and eventually found he was getting very positive results throughout the 1950s regressing patients back to their perinatal period—from conception to birth. It was only after he met and married Joan Grant that he started to use past-life regression as another therapeutic tool. Joan was an author and psychic who had an unusual ability to spontaneously recall the past lives of her subjects. Their collaborative effort produced the book *Many Lifetimes* which was published in 1967. The chapters alternate between Grant and Kelsey as they present their experiences using past-life regression with the guidance of psychic information provided by Joan. Many interesting therapeutically oriented cases are presented as they delineate a model of how past-life experiences play themselves out in current lives. They touch on the importance of the past-life death experience in energizing issues brought forward as well as the influence of the perinatal period in transferring those issues from the past. With all of their certainty about reincarnation, they make it clear that this technique, as effective and quick as it can be, is not a cure–all, and in fact past lives do not account for all issues facing a client.

The Recent History of Past-Life Regression Therapy

In the late 60s and early 70s several more books came out which continued to document the past-life antecedents of current life problems. The latter half of the 1970s would see publications by practitioners and therapists with more attention to methods, techniques, and scientific verification.

In her 1976 book *Hypersentience*, Marcia Moore makes the critical point that it is less important whether past-life recollections are genuine than whether they are actual communications from the unconscious mind. Such communications Moore concluded "enable people to open the eye to their inner vision" and "aspire to more exalted states of being."[3]

In 1978 and 1979 four books were published by professional psychotherapists that would establish the final foundation for the field of past-

---

[3]Marcia Moore, *Hypersentience* (New York: Bantam Books, 1976), xii.

life therapy. Perhaps the classics regarding valid research in the field are the works of Helen Wambach, PhD. Her first book entitled *Reliving Past Lives* presents her personal story regarding the discovery of the process of past-life recall as a psychotherapeutic technique under hypnosis. She reported that regardless of the current sex, subjects have a 50-50 ratio of male-to-female lives. Concerning socioeconomic class, over 70 percent of lives are in lower classes and characteristics such as race, clothing, footwear, and even dishware used corresponded to historical data. She also verified that the experience around death tended to be the root cause of presenting issues in current life.

It was her second book, *Life Before Life*, that took a slightly different approach to the research. In this study she asks specific questions about the perinatal period and the time of birth. She writes of some fascinating results that correspond to other more esoteric sources such as the Cayce readings. The choice of whether or not to be born, for example, and the circumstances of the forthcoming life are decided with the help of counselors in the before-life state. The research clearly indicates that the purpose of life is to learn lessons and to enhance relationships. Before her death in 1988, Helen Wambach would start some fascinating research on the progression into future lives which was to be carried on by Dr. Chet Snow and published in 1990. Although that book adds little to the technique of past-life regression therapy, it does provide inspiring insight into the power of the unconscious mind and the use of progression techniques in working with terminally ill clients or those with a fear of death.

The next significant piece of work in the late 70s was written by Edith Fiore, PhD. Dr. Fiore was a California psychotherapist who wrote about two years of experience using past-life regression under hypnosis as a primary therapeutic approach. In the book *You Have Been Here Before*, she discusses nine cases which resulted in the successful resolution of issues like obesity, sexual dysfunction, migraines, and insomnia. After almost nine more years of practice and teaching, Dr. Fiore published *The Unquiet Dead*. This would become a pioneering body of work as it concludes that spirit possession accounts for a good percentage of the dysfunctional behavior and discomfort we feel in the normal course of life. She documents the theory and techniques behind what she calls "depossession therapy."

The third book to appear in 1978 was authored by Morris Netherton, PhD and Nancy Schiffrin. In *Past Lives Therapy* a technique is defined that is markedly different from the standard hypnotic induction and processing techniques used by other practitioners to date. Netherton believes that the unconscious mind never shuts down and is always picking up input from the environment even while under anesthesia and other episodes of unconsciousness. For Netherton the perinatal period is another critical time when the information is taken into the unconscious process. He is one of the first to emphasize that past-life traumas are part of a chain of experiences connected with the perinatal and biographical life which reinforce the presenting behavior or issue— or complex. And he believes that hypnosis actually interferes with the complete uncovering and release of a complex. For this reason, his technique calls for the repetition of the trigger phrases and words associated with the traumatic experiences that initiated the complex in order to relive the experiences. It is the process of re-experiencing all of these aspects throughout the past life, perinatal, and biographical life that creates the healing effect. Aside from cases involving phobias, sexual dysfunction, alcoholism, relationship conflicts, and hyperactivity, Netherton presents several successful cases dealing with physical disorders and even diseases like epilepsy, ulcers, and cancer. The Netherton technique made a major contribution to the field of past-life therapy, especially regarding my own approach which we'll talk about in Chapter Five.

The work of Wambach, Fiore, and Netherton set the stage for a groundswell of movement in the field in the 1980s. The decade opened with a meeting of fifty-two psychotherapists at a University of California conference to discuss the establishment of a professional organization. The Association for Past-Life Research and Therapy (APRT) was formed to act as a central agency for the dissemination of information supporting the advancement of the field. In 1986 *The Journal for Regression Therapy* was first published, and the organization started to host annual conferences and trainings to encourage and monitor proficiency in the field. That organization has evolved into an international agency which continues to pursue its professional mission.

Between 1981 and 1986 five books were published by practitioners and researchers in the field which continued to raise interest among the general public and the professional mental health community. It was 1987 that saw two significant works hit the bookstores. One was by Karl Schlotterbeck, a student of Morris Netherton. Entitled *Living Your Past Lives*, it presented a nice overview of the heritage of reincarnation thinking along with the metaphysical model that supported the therapeutic effects of the regression work.

The second book of the year—*Other Lives, Other Selves*—might well be considered a classic in the field. As a Jungian therapist and an admirer of Netherton, the author Roger Woolger, PhD presented perhaps the most comprehensive treatment of field for the general reader as well as the professional. Woolger presents a new perspective as he emphasizes the concept of the physical–mental–spiritual connection, the idea of the archetypal influence on past-life experiences, and the playing through of past-life subpersonalities in the current life. His technique focuses on processing past-life experiences with the idea of finishing the unfinished business of those times much like the techniques in Gestalt therapy, psychodrama, and the Netherton approach. Essentially, this cathartic, experiential technique involves revisiting prior times—past lives and the between-life state (the Bardo state)—and reprocessing the traumatic experiences in a way that resolves the associated feelings and reactions. Woolger's technique also pays attention to the discharge of the physical sensations resulting from those experiences.

With Roger Woolger's book gaining popularity, 1988 saw the release of another book that would stimulate even more popular interest. Brian Weiss, MD, a respected psychiatrist and researcher, released *Many Lives, Many Masters* about his personal introduction to the technique. He talks about the case of Catherine who experienced a spontaneous past-life memory while under hypnosis to treat a severe phobia. It was through a series of regressions that he became a believer in not only the efficacy of the technique but the concept of reincarnation. According to Dr. Weiss, what finally convinced him that the source of the memories where from a higher level of consciousness was when Catherine actually channeled personal information for him. *Many Lives, Many Masters* generated more attention to the field than any other book to date. Weiss went on the publish several other books which are still in print, including *Only Love Is Real, Messages from The Masters; Meditation: Achieving Inner Peace and Tranquility in Your Life;* and *Same Soul, Many Bodies.* His recent appearance on Oprah continues to keep Dr. Weiss and past-life regression therapy in the minds of the general public.

The momentum generated during the 1980s certainly carried over into the nineties and through the turn of the century. Books authored by psychotherapists and researchers continued to appear. In fact, since the year 2000, some fourteen books have been published espousing the techniques and results of exploring past lives for healing and growth.

This brief history lesson makes it clear that the therapeutic technique of recalling past lives grew up right alongside of modern psychology. In fact, there is documentation that the therapeutic effects of revisiting past-life experiences were recognized even before Wilhelm Wundt and Sigmund Freud started their work. What is also obvious in this history and in the more recent publications is that the emphasis of past-life regression as a therapeutic technique has been on uncovering and releasing the negative themes or complexes that disrupt our lives. However, the karmic logic, as reinforced by the Cayce readings, clearly indicates that not only negative complexes carry forward but also positive complexes that can converge into a soul purpose theme. For this reason, our primary mission in this book is to enable you to not only address the negative complexes in this self-help approach but to also emphasize those past-life experiences that form the positive karmic patterns, complexes, talents, skills, and ways of being that are carried into this life. As mentioned earlier, we'll also explore how these positive themes, in one form or another, are vehicles for the realization of that unique sense of soul purpose.

Important Points in This Chapter

▶ Reincarnation thinking has been a prominent concept throughout history—not only in the Eastern religions but in primitive cultures, early Western philosophies, and even in the early days of our Western Mosaic religions of Judaism, Christianity, and Islam.

▶ The intuited psychic readings of Edgar Cayce validate the idea that we carry into this life positive and negative karmic patterns as well as a unique sense of soul purpose and that we decide which of these patterns to bring into this life before conception.

▶ The exploration of past–life regression as a therapeutic technique predates the development of modern psychology.

▶ Throughout this history the clinical healing benefits have been the impetus for the research and development of this technique.

▶ Belief in reincarnation is not necessary for the subject to experience the benefits.

▶ The Bridey Murphy case validated the credibility of past–life memories.

▶ The experiences surrounding the death in a given life are the root cause of presenting issues.

▶ The presenting issues may have to do with physical as well as behavioral and psycho–emotional disorders.

▶ What is most helpful is not only to observe the past–life experiences but also to finish the unfinished business of the past by reprocessing those experiences.

▶ Recollections of the perinatal experiences as well as past lives were important in providing insight and a healing effect.

▶ The before–life state is where critical decisions regarding the coming life are made.

▶ Integrated Imagery makes use of all of these concepts by considering not only the negative but also the positive karmic patterns, the issue of soul purpose, and the energetic chain of experience.

An Exercise to Continue Your Awakening Process

In this exercise you'll have the opportunity to use your psychic intuition to start to awaken memories of your past lives by exploring geographic locations and periods of history that are most pronounced for you.

Prepare for the exercise:
• When you're ready, find a quiet and comfortable place where you can relax and reflect on your past–life history.

- Have your journal and any drawing materials with you.
- Have your CD player and the enclosed CD available to guide you through the exercise.
- Prepare to listen to Track One on the CD with my voice guiding you through the progressive relaxation exercise.
- The transcript for Track One is in Appendix B.
- Set the Intention to:
  - Move above your body—above your house—above the town where you live—above the country.
  - Move above the Earth until you can start to move around and view all of the countries and regions on the Earth.
  - Notice which of these geographic locations and countries or cities you're drawn to the most in a positive way. Which are you repulsed by?
  - Before you come back to this time, be aware of any periods in history or religious traditions that are the most prominent.
  - When you're ready, come back to this time and place. Journal your insights.

Start the exercise:
- Close your eyes and take several deep, relaxing breaths.
- Start the CD.
- Stop the CD when you've finished the progressive relaxation exercise.
- Start your journey.

When you feel you have finished, just open your eyes and come back fully refreshed and relaxed. Take a few quiet moments to reflect on what you've experienced. What impressions do you have about this history or these geographic locations? What insights have you had? Is there a particular idea or period in history that you resonate more—or less—with? Are there particular events or characters in history that you are more—or less—attracted to? Take some time to journal your insights and impressions.

Chapter **2**

Edgar Cayce on Reincarnation and Soul Purpose

The life of Edgar Cayce is an extraordinary episode in the history of reincarnation thinking. He helped thousands of people through his readings and remedies. The spiritual insights and metaphysical system that came out of those readings remains an inspiration for anyone seeking purpose and well-being in this life. This system provides any serious student of reincarnation philosophy—or anyone interested in experiencing past–life regression—valuable road maps not only for understanding the influence and effect of past experiences on his/her current life but also the concept and process of soul development. For our purposes we'll use the philosophy out of the Cayce readings as a guideline for the Integrated Imagery exercises in this book and your personal journey of self–discovery.

Let's take a moment to review why this system can be helpful and why I have used the philosophy found in the readings as a foundation for the technique of Integrated Imagery. The readings clearly indicate how traumatic experiences and transgressions in past lives are carried forward into this life. As important is the explanation of how positive experiences, talents, abilities, and ways of being are repeated and continued in this life. In addition they address how these positive aspects of ourselves can be the seeds of a unique sense of soul purpose. The readings also talk about the soul's experience in the between–life and the before–life states in terms of clarifying and understanding the impact of past-life experiences. They explain that on a soul level we decide what the issues and opportunities are that we will deal with in this life. These insights verify the importance of the different aspects of the energetic chain of experience and the benefit of accessing those states of consciousness in the process of Integrated Imagery. In the course of a Cayce reading, his subjects were provided an explanation of their karmic history. Through the Integrated Imagery exercises that follow, you will have the opportunity not only to understand but also to process your own karmic past.

The Creation Story

A good place to start to understand the philosophy that is the basis of the readings is with the creation story or the explanation of the origin of human kind and its spiritual aspect. This story helps to explain the purpose of reincarnation and the issue of spiritual evolution. According to the readings and an interpretation in *The Essential Edgar Cayce* by Mark Thurston, PhD, one of the leading Cayce scholars today, God created all of the souls in the universe at once as sparks or emanations of Him/Herself. Modern science might refer to these emanations as holograms. The purpose was to provide God with co-creative companionship that would be individual and free and yet a part of the original whole that was God. In simple terms, we were created with God-like powers and the potential to emulate God, to become one with God, and to experience our interconnectedness while still maintaining our sense of individuality. Our spiritual path then involves reconnecting with that true nature, our higher selves, and moving on to states, experiences, or regions beyond, whether we call these regions nirvana, atman, or heaven. With the power of free will, each incarnation on this path is an opportunity to learn new lessons, develop skills, and fine tune our ability to connect with our higher natures. Unfortunately, along this path most souls have lost their way. We have developed positive patterns, skills, talents, and ways of being, but we have also created negative patterns in wrong doing, wrong thinking, and wrong feeling. These positive and negative patterns also become a part of our soul energy which we carry forward along our path from incarnation to incarnation. These positive and negative complexes or karmic patterns (as the readings indicate) play a key role in our purpose and progress in a given lifetime on the earth plane, and they become the focus of the process of past-life therapy.

At this point, one specific reading provides a fine example of the interplay of karma, soul purpose, and spiritual development. A couple brought their eleven-year-old son to Cayce for a health reading. The child had developed a severe case of bed-wetting which was not showing signs of subsiding. During the course of the reading Cayce spontaneously moved into a life reading. The reading indicated that the child's soul purpose was to develop as a spiritual leader through the arts but that unless the bed-wetting was stopped, the child's self-image would be so damaged that he would never accomplish his mission. The indication was that the child had been a preacher in New England and that he had sought out "possessed" children and organized dunking as punishment. Cayce suggests that at the end of this lifetime, the soul during its life review had realized the error in this witch dunking and experienced a great sense of guilt for these wrongs. In the current twentieth century life time, this guilt was now being enacted as a symbolic dunking of oneself through the bedwetting. In other words, this child brought with him the karmic complex created by those witch-dunking activities that could potentially interfere with a higher purpose in his current life. In this case the child was affected by a physical disorder that interfered with his soul purpose. This negative karmic complex could very well have been an emotional or psychological disorder that unconsciously creates circumstances that make life challenging. In any case, the work is to deal with these challenging complexes while pursuing one's soul purpose—all in the process of returning to or realizing one's interconnectedness with God.

Ideals and Soul Purpose

There are a few more points that are helpful to know in our self-discovery process. The Cayce readings indicate that the soul has the opportunity in the purely spiritual, between life-state not only to review the past-life experiences and lessons, but also to preview and plan the next incarnation. The choice of parents, geographic location, and even the astrological birth chart may be part of the plan. It is at this point that the soul establishes a soul mission or a purpose for that next life. As described by Dr. Mark Thurston, the soul—like the gem cutter—is faced with a multifaceted, rough-cut gem to polish and perfect. In each life it chooses one aspect of the gem to polish until all the facets are eventually polished. Each life, then, may carry a different soul mission until the final destination is reached—until all the cosmic (spiritual) lessons are learned and all of the negative karmic complexes are resolved.

More specifically, this soul mission, then, is a way of being, a spirit, or a feeling about life. It is not the goal (e.g. to become president) but the spirit in which one chooses to live a life (e.g. to provide guidance and leadership to a nation). It is a spiritual pattern or imprint for how and for what purpose a life is to be led. Dr. Herbert Puryear puts it another way in his book *The Cayce Primer* where he describes an ideal or soul mission as a "motivational standard by which to evaluate our goals and our reasons for pursuing those goals."[4]

Taking one step back to the creation story, the ultimate overall goal for all of us is to achieve Oneness or companionship with God. It comes with a sense of a universal love and what the readings define as Christ Consciousness. The ideal, mission, or soul purpose for a given incarnation, then, is a lesser step in that direction. An example in a given life might be service to others, nurturing of self, care for the environment, sensitivity to the unenlightened, or any number of ways of being that involve some interaction of self with others. In any case, it sets the pattern for that life so that lessons may be learned, negative complexes

---

[4]Herbert Puryear, *The Edgar Cayce Primer* (New York: Bantam, 1982), 36.

may be resolved, positive themes may be utilized, and the soul may progress on its journey.

It is clear throughout the readings that the ideal or soul purpose may be fulfilled in several ways. For example, if my ideal were to provide enabling guidance and service to others, I might go to the extent of building a spiritual center and making a career out of spiritual counseling. On the other hand, volunteering time to lend spiritual support and guidance to others or simply developing a state of mind and the habit of helping and enabling anyone I met would fulfill that same life mission. How one fulfills his/her soul purpose is then left to the free will of the individual.

It is important to reiterate here the point made earlier that although the ideal may be tied to lessons, it should not be confused with or complicated by negative karmic patterns. In any given life one may come in with a set of negative karmic patterns or complexes to deal with because of past-life experiences. Just as with the eleven-year-old bed-wetter, the key is to release oneself from the karmic complexes or lessons so that fulfillment through achievement of life mission is possible. The major objectives of awakening past lives are to release oneself from these negative complexes which are educative and to enliven and facilitate the process of living one's life mission or soul purpose.

Examples of Soul Purpose Themes

To help motivate the undeveloped to mature.

To celebrate the workings of God through nature
and to appreciate and cultivate nature.

To synthesize and blend.

The innovator—getting new things started.

To be a builder, a finisher who sees things through to completion.

Sensitivity and support for the less fortunate ones in life.

To bring hope to others.

To provide enabling guidance to those on a spiritual path.

To nurture my own spiritual development through
an active spiritual practice and by helping others.

To support, guide, and nurture the development of children.

To demonstrate the workings of spirit through my work.

To inspire the spiritual development of others through the arts.

Important Points in This Chapter

▶ The metaphysical system in the Cayce readings is a valuable road map to understanding reincarnation and karma.

▶ The readings explain how traumatic experiences and transgressions in past lives are directly and indirectly carried into this life.

▶ Positive experiences are also continued or repeated from past lives.

▶ Each of us has a unique soul purpose to fulfill in this life.

▶ In the between-life and before-life states we make decisions as to the karmic patterns, lessons, and soul purpose we will pursue in the coming life.

▶ Our souls are emanations from God.

▶ On a soul level our mission is to realize our Oneness with God.

▶ Life is about accentuating the positive and resolving (de-energizing) the negative.

An Exercise to Start Your Exploration of Soul Purpose

In this exercise you'll be taking the first step in clarifying or perhaps uncovering for the first time your true sense of soul purpose.

Prepare for the exercise:
- When you're ready, again find a quiet and comfortable place where you can relax and reflect on insights regarding your soul purpose.
- Have your journal and drawing materials at hand.
- Review your autobiographical time line and reflect on experiences in your life or periods of your life when you felt joy and a passion for what you were doing.
- Use Track One on the enclosed CD to guide you through the progressive relaxation exercise.

- Set the intention of uncovering or validating a primary theme in your life that might have to do with what you know so far about the idea of soul purpose.

Start the exercise:
- Close your eyes and take several deep relaxing breaths.
- Start the CD
- Stop the CD when you've finished the progressive relaxation exercise.
- In your mind's eye start to reflect on your life, your experiences, and your relationships.
- Which activities and experiences have given you the most pleasure? Do they have to do with your work life, your leisure time, or your relationships?
- Before you come back, imagine yourself sometime in the future living your ideal day. Think outside the box; there are no restrictions. How are you spending your day or week? Who accompanies you? Where do you live? What kind of work do you do? How do you spend your time?

When you feel you have finished, just open your eyes and come back fully refreshed and relaxed. Take a few more quiet moments to reflect on your experience and journal your insights.

Chapter **3**

The Laws of Karma

In this chapter it's time to take a more definitive look at the mechanism of karma and how past–life and between–life experiences play through into our current lives. What exactly do we carry forward from these prior times? How do actions from the past relate to each other in the way we pursue relationships and the activities of life? How do these past–life experiences affect us psychologically, emotionally, and physically? Do we have a choice in the matter or is all of this out of our control? What's the purpose of all of this? It's all too easy to rest on the impression that karma is purely punitive—having to do with wrong acts in the past that are antecedents of difficult, challenging experiences in the present. Most people seem to have this simplistic definition in mind that karma is purely about cause and effect. There's a lot more to it than that.

To put all of this into perspective, let's go back to some basics. We've established that life is about growth, development, or evolution on a soul level. In one form or another all of the spiritual belief systems that embrace the idea of reincarnation adhere to this single principle. This is clearly the central focus of the Cayce readings as well. We have even seen the idea of soul development validated in thousands of case studies published by the leading past-life therapists and researchers. This is our starting point. So this whole process of living and reliving has a purpose and a plan, and we can start to see how the agenda in each life fits into that plan. The soul development explanation makes it important for us to consider that not only negative but also positive experiences, complexes, and patterns from the past affect our day-to-day lives. Equally important, as emphasized in the Cayce readings, is the idea that we carry a unique sense of soul purpose or life mission into each life.

The Edgar Cayce Readings on Karma

To get a more specific idea of the workings of karma, let's look at the work of a few scholars on the subject. Gina Cerminara, PhD, is one of the earliest professional authors on the readings of Edgar Cayce. In *Many Mansions* and several other books, she defines the terrain of karma—comparable to Hindu beliefs—as explained in the life readings. She describes karma as working on the principle of cause and effect or antecedent and consequence, whereby any given act will be the cause of a compensating act. If we, for example, perform an act that inflicts pain on another, we set up a negative karmic pattern which must be balanced. One point that is clear is that there is not necessarily a reciprocal effect or consequence to the initial act or cause; in other words, if I murder you in a past-life, you won't necessarily murder me in this life. The implication being that there is more of a purpose to karma than simply "an eye-for-an-eye" debt repayment or punishment. There is, in fact, an educative aspect.

To help understand the more complex version, let's look at karma in line with the Law of Oneness of the universe. As the readings suggest and Dr. Cerminara emphasizes, the universe is a balanced, living structure composed of thought forms or energy patterns (masses of vibrations coming together in different configurations to form solids, energy, and thought patterns). These aspects of the universe are created by God and our individual souls which emanate from God. If an imbalance occurs through a negative act, then it must be compensated for and rebalanced. A negative self-oriented act like inflicting pain or suffering must be balanced by a positive act. It seems fair that the individual soul who caused the problem should resolve it. But remember, this system of the universe is driven by the principle of Oneness. The idea of love, growth, and reawakening to our original states of attunement with God is the name of the game. So what we have is not necessarily debt repayment or punishment for the sake of punishment but an opportunity to balance the asymmetry and to learn some lesson that relates to the progression toward Oneness. Karma then allows for an educative experience set up for each of us to learn the lessons we need in order to become worthy of co-creatorship with God.

According to Cayce—and Cerminara—the karmic patterns or complexes we all face today are derived from two sources. One set of karmic patterns originated during the soul's excursion through the universe prior to becoming entangled in the earth plane. During that period we all had free will to create and to interact in whatever way we chose. Consequently positive and negative experiences started to set up positive and negative karmic patterns or complexes. Finally, God confined us to the earth plane—what the Cayce readings refer to as "the fall"—in order to facilitate the process of soul growth which now also involved balancing the negative patterns. As we kept on incarnating from lifetime to lifetime in the earth plane, we continued to exhibit negative behaviors and thought patterns. We continued to rack up out-of-balance negative karma. So the overall soul project now involves exercising our free will to have experiences that lead us to the realization of our true connection with God which may be called the unitive nature. This involves compensating for or overcoming the negative patterns we have created for ourselves through successive lifetimes.

To consider karma strictly in negative terms is by no means accurate. In fact, karma has a positive aspect to it which is not only comforting but also supportive of soul development. As suggested, just as negative patterns are carried forward from one life to another so are positive patterns. One who develops a talent or skill may have access to that talent or skill in future lifetimes. For that matter, any positive behavior or act like a life of service to others creates a positive karmic pattern that may be enjoyed in future times. To get a better idea of the complexity of karmic process, let's go back into Dr. Cerminara's explanation of karmic laws in the readings.

She describes the two aspects of karma as retributive and continuitive. In retributive karma there is the element of debt repayment, but again with another purpose in mind than simply vengeance. Using the physical body as an example, retributive karma can manifest in a number of ways. One case in point is the "boomerang effect" where there is an identical rebound of negative behavior as with the paraplegic who in a past life as a prison keeper would cripple his prisoners for the fun of it. There is the gluttonous behavior in one life that results in severe digestive problems in another. In the symbolic effect under retributive karma, there is a much different consequence of former life behavior. The political official in one life who turns a deaf ear to cries for help in a given life ends up deaf himself in another life. Or the one who needlessly sheds blood in one life suffers from an anemic condition in another.

Continuitive karma, on the other hand, has other implications. The mechanism by which it operates involves the continuation of behavioral, attitudinal, and thought patterns, both negative and positive, as long as some thrust or energy is applied to them. In this respect, years of study to develop a skill in music or art can show results which can continue into subsequent lives. A life of dedication and service to others will be rewarded in future times. The principle of continuity is especially comforting when we consider that no positive act or work right up to the moment of death will be lost or unrewarded. In fact, continuity alone explains the phenomenon of the child prodigy like Mozart who brings into a life an already developed talent. But there is the dark side of this principle. A life or lives spent allowing persecutors to have their way can result in a current life of continued persecution. For that matter, several lives involving the persecution of others or self-deprecation can result in those behaviors carrying on in this life.

Lynn Sparrow, in her 1988 book *Reincarnation: Claiming Your Past, Creating Your Future*, adds another important dimension to Cerminara's interpretation of the Cayce readings regarding karmic process. In her Law of

Continuation she also emphasizes the purposeful need to invest ongoing energy into a positive characteristic or behavior in order to keep it going in subsequent lifetimes. With the Law of Consequences corresponding to Cerminara's idea of retributive karma, she stresses the point that there are consequences not only to negative behaviors and experiences but also to positive behaviors in a given past life. All of this corresponds with the idea of balancing any negative energy and learning lessons associated with the state of Oneness as opposed to purely a punitive reaction.

It is Sparrow's description of the Law of Positive Returns that draws another perspective from the Cayce readings. In this principle any positive behavior is not only equally compensated for but in fact, may be returned many fold. One simple act of kindness may result in a lifetime on the receiving end. One sincere and unselfish act of love may bring a lifetime of loving support and encouragement.

Some Key Points to Remember in the Cayce Readings

There are several principles out of the readings that are worth repeating. These are rules that are helpful in understanding what drives the process of karma. They are also very important to consider as you pursue your own journey of self-discovery. One is that in the between-life and before-life states the soul exists in a different dimension of consciousness. This state allows reflection on the experiences and lessons of past lives and provides an opportunity to exercise free will in planning the circumstances of the next life. It is here that we may select parents, friends, and other relationships. Positive and negative karmic complexes may be chosen as part of the mission of the next life. Even the overall soul purpose of the next life may be selected. The readings also clearly indicate that specific physical characteristics and even astrological configurations may be selected to provide the appropriate setting for the learning of lessons and the pursuit of soul purpose. Considering that we have a say in the planning process and we have free will in how we respond in the life experience, we are assured in the readings that we will never have more than we can handle in a given life.

There is another principle that interestingly enough relates to the concept of the Boddhisattva in Buddhism. The Cayce readings indicate that once we complete our earthly lessons or complete our karmic process, we then move on to even higher dimensions of consciousness in this process of soul development. Even then we have the freedom to reincarnate simply to be of service to others. In the readings the idea is emphasized that none of us truly enters the gates of heaven until we all stand at the door. Clearly, this process of soul development then is a collective process which makes sense considering the idea that we are all emanations of the same God and remain interconnected.

There is one other key principle in the Cayce philosophy that is important to consider. Even with the opportunity to choose the circumstances of a given life and the idea that karma is not punitive, it's all too easy to think of this process of reincarnation as mechanical, merciless, and overwhelming. It is the Law of Grace in the readings that can eliminate these concerns. Grace promises that karma does not have to be met in the ways that we fear most. Grace is the gift of God which allows us to focus on our lessons and not be concerned with guilt or punishment. In essence, it allows us to dismiss lifetimes of karma with nothing more than a sincere expression of repentance for past transgressions or the realization of sincere appreciation for the reality of our interconnection with God and with each other. It doesn't require that we repay debt equivalently but only that we truly realize the lesson to be learned. Grace can come during moments of critical need or in life's lesser crises. It comes in the moments when our prayers are answered for the comfort of someone else, when we sincerely acknowledge our mistakes, or when in a moment of desperation we realize an unexplainable sense of comfort and strength. As we continue on this journey of awakening, it will be important to remember this principle is not only present in the Cayce readings but in most spiritual belief systems. The Law of Grace, then, provides all of us the opportunity to release or complete some karmic patterns and to accentuate others on this path of soul development simply by realizing our true nature as creative emanations of God.

The Work of Hans TenDam

Before we go on, it's important to touch on the work of another past-life regression researcher. Hans TenDam, in his 1987 book *Exploring Reincarnation*, presents one of the most extensive overviews of reincarnation philosophy, past-life regression therapy, and karma to date. In several key chapters he discusses the many aspects and debates regarding karma as reflected in the most significant spiritual systems and in the research findings of those who practice regression therapy. What results is an even more definitive description of the workings of karma with regard to what experiences or patterns are carried forward, why they become aspects of current lives, and how the whole process is controlled.

TenDam starts by describing four general reasons for reincarnating–*natural, educative, volitional,* and *mission.* These are the reasons that drive the process of reincarnation.

First is the idea that reincarnation happens according to *natural* laws or what he calls *causal* patterns without input or control by the incarnating soul or guides. He describes how this natural or causal mechanism of karma seems to work based on the results of not only past–life regression researchers but also the expansive literature from the various spiritual traditions. He starts by breaking down these causal patterns of karma into retention, repercussion, and fruition. These patterns may be thought of as an inadvertent mechanism of transfer in that there is no apparent purposeful plan except that the energy in the complex needs to be balanced in the case of a negative complex and activated in the case of a positive one. The incarnating soul, as well, has absolutely no control over the patterns brought into a life.

More specifically, retention involves the transfer of abilities, talents, tendencies, feelings, and physical characteristics. A talent in debating, in the arts, or in speaking a language, for example, may be carried forward from a past life. Emotions like self–confidence or a feeling of inferiority may be inadvertently retained just as a body type or even a relationship from the past. In any of these scenarios one may retain either a positive or a negative pattern, characteristic, or circumstance.

Repercussion, on the other hand, refers to undigested or unresolved patterns, involving trauma that result in postulates, scripts, fears, or obsessions. As we'll see in the next section, these repercussive patterns become a part of negative complexes that carry feelings, images, scripts, sensations, and behaviors that were formed in past lives. In this way a violent rape in a former life may result in a non-orgasmic sex life or severe lower back problems. A life of poverty may result in a feeling of fear about being destitute and a dysfunctional drive to overachieve in terms of the accumulation of wealth. Postulates develop in similar ways out of traumatic experiences, but with a semantic reaction. "I will never show my emotions again"; "I'll never fall in love again"; "I can never measure up," or "Nothing good ever happens to me" are just some of the charged statements that go on in our heads and can even play through in conscious speech. These postulates are the scripts that affect other behaviors and set up oversensitivities to the common experiences of life. Once again, these repercussive patterns are totally unplanned prior to the life and are a result of repressed or unfinished business forming out of traumatic experiences.

The third causal pattern of karma is fruition which directly correlates with Lynn Sparrow's ideas of *positive returns* in the Cayce readings. Through fruition one reaps the positive or negative benefits of an investment of energy. A long personal relationship with someone—positive or negative—may lead to a continuation of that relationship or at least the feelings of love, mistrust, companionship, etc., that are associated with that person. Abilities and other activities may also be carried on in subsequent lives. Practice leads to development; neglect leads to atrophy and backsliding. Several lives spent developing a talent as a painter can result in an inborn talent for the visual arts. TenDam uses many examples like this to make the point that under these causal patterns an active life of struggling with one's talents and personal development may reap benefits in subsequent lives. By the same token, passive negative behavioral patterns in a given life may lead to more of the same in current life.

The second of TenDam's reasons for reincarnating is *educational* in that the purpose of the current life is to learn chosen lessons within the context of a life plan. A soul in this case may have some degree of say in determining the life circumstances and soul purpose in the current life.

In this case in the before-life state, the soul may choose to retain some prior characteristic or pattern or bring in the repercussive effects or negative complexes from a prior life. The obvious difference here is that the choice is up to the individual incarnating soul, and the purpose is focused on learning lessons and soul development. The same principles of retention, repercussion, and fruition may apply in this educational approach but now with a purposeful decision before the incarnation and a life plan.

The third of TenDam's reasons for reincarnating is *volitional*. This reason also involves a life plan but now with absolute freedom to choose the circumstances of the current life. The difference here is that the circumstances need not be based on learning as much as on personal desires, needs, and preferences. In this case, I may choose to suspend working on any negative karma and draw on my positive inventory of prior experiences to focus on living a life of leisure or creativity—a life surrounded by nature and the animal world or a fulfilling life involving a successful career with close friends and family. This reincarnation experience is comparable to Lynn Sparrow's interpretation of the Law of Continuation and the Law of Positive Returns where the incarnating soul has the opportunity to take advantage of the accumulation of positive karma.

Finally, TenDam talks about *mission* as a fourth reason for reincarnating. In this case the life plan has to do only with the idea of service to others and a contribution to society. This scenario then directly corresponds to the idea emphasized in the Cayce readings and the Boddhisattva life indicated in Buddhism. As Cayce describes, this is usually when the soul has completed all of its lessons in the earth plane or has resolved all karma and decides to return with the expressed purpose of service to others. In TenDam's interpretation the choice to live a life purely dedicated to mission can come at any time, regardless of the level of soul development. Here we can see how a life of service to others may still have the effect of balancing negative karma even on a collective level although the purpose in this case is selfless and for the good of humanity.

An Important Note

What I've tried to do in this chapter is to give you a better under-standing of how this sometimes complicated process of karma works. What experiences and imprints do we carry from our past lives? How do these imprints play out in our biographical lives? Why do we bring into this life specific themes and purpose? These laws of karma should be considered nothing more than guidelines. As you continue on your own journey of self-discovery and awakening, be flexible when connecting the dotted lines from past lives to this life. Above all, it's important to simply trust your unconscious mind regarding the stories and insights that appear.

Important Points in This Chapter

- Karma works on the principle of antecedent and consequence, whereby any given act will be the cause of a compensating act.
- There is more to karma than the idea of debt repayment or pun-ishment–there is an educative factor.
- The Law of Oneness of the universe is a basic principle that ex-plains the drive to balance actions in the material plane.
- Cerminara explains the two aspects of karma as retributive and continuitive.
- In retributive karma we have the "boomerang effect" and the "sym-bolic effect."
- Continuitive karma results in the continuation of positive and negative behavioral, attitudinal, and thought patterns.
- Lynn Sparrow talks about the Law of Continuation and the Law of Consequences.
- She also talks about the Law of Positive Returns where positive behavior may be returned many fold.
- Again, the Cayce readings reinforce the idea that we have free will in choosing the karmic patterns to be brought into the coming life.
- We also have the choice to come into a life with the sole purpose of being of service to others.

▶ The Law of Grace in the readings allows the opportunity to release all karmic patterns simply by realizing our true nature.

▶ TenDam talks about four reasons for reincarnation–natural, educative, volitional, and mission.

An Exercise to Start to Explore Your Karma

Considering that our karmic patterns carry into this life and continue to replay throughout our lives, this exercise will allow you to start to explore how some of these have affected your biographical experience in positive and negative ways.

Prepare for the exercise:
- Again, retreat to your quiet place; have your journal and time line at hand.
- Review and reflect on what you've recorded so far on your time line.
- Use Track One on the enclosed CD to guide you through the progressive relaxation exercise.
- Set the intention of the repeating experiences in your life and the consequences of those experiences.

Start the exercise:
- Close your eyes and take several deep, relaxing breaths.
- Start the CD.
- Stop the CD when you've finished the progressive relaxation exercise.
- In your mind's eye, start to reflect on:
  - Positive experiences, actions, and thoughts that have resulted in positive consequences.
  - Negative experiences, actions, and thoughts that have resulted in negative consequences and repercussions.
  - How these positive or negative experiences, action, or thoughts have become a theme in your life.
  - How positive experiences, actions, and thoughts have had not only positive but also expansive results.

When you feel you've finished, just open your eyes and come back fully refreshed and relaxed. Take a few more quiet moments to reflect on your experience, and journal your insights.

Chapter **4**

Integrated Imagery

There are several characteristics of Integrated Imagery that are common to other approaches of past-life regression mentioned in Chapter One. It is a regression technique using hypnosis and altered states of consciousness to access memories of the past. In the process it enables the therapist to guide the client/subject back into past lives that relate to current life circumstances. Finally, it enables one to explore those past-life memories that are at the core of the dysfunctional karmic patterns which tend to disrupt one's current life.

There are, however, several features of Integrated Imagery that distinguish it as a psychotherapeutic technique with a spiritual perspective. As the title indicates, it is an integrated approach which incorporates traditional and some non-traditional therapeutic techniques. In this way, it considers and makes use of the methods and techniques from all four of the movements in modern psychology. Cognitive, behavioral, and contemporary psychoanalytical approaches as much as the principles in the fields of humanistic and transpersonal psychology are all in one form or another integrated into the Integrated Imagery process. Some of the techniques in Gestalt therapy, psychodrama, and Ericksonian hypnosis are also incorporated in the way prior memories are accessed and processed.

In this respect, it is an experiential therapeutic approach that enables the subject to reexperience the trauma or traumatic history of an issue so as not only to uncover the root cause experience but also to complete, reprocess, and essentially finish the unfinished business of the past. To feel what was not felt, say what was not said, do what was not done in the course of the formation of those karmic patterns or themes in past lives.

It is also integrated in that the approach, regardless of the therapeutic objective (or the diagnosis), always calls for the consideration and uncovering of the positive as well as the negative aspects and history of the subject. As we've seen, our positive karmic themes, skills, talents, and ways of being are also born in the past. The importance of awakening the past-life experiences at the root of our positive complexes has some significant implications. For one, it enables us to reinforce and enliven those positive aspects of ourselves in our biographical lives. Mary, in the introduction, was able to validate and more effectively act on those positive aspects of herself that she was already aware of. This regression process can also serve to bring to awareness and enliven positive attributes and karmic patterns that were unrecognized. The integration of the positive and negative karmic patterns also serves an important purpose in revealing the interactive dynamics of those past experiences and the resulting karmic patterns or complexes.

Another important distinction is that this regression technique approaches the process of psycho-emotional and psycho-spiritual healing with the idea that there is a body/mind connection. In other words, all of our psychological and spiritual issues and blessings have a physical component to them. These karmic patterns, in one way or another, are imprinted in the physical body. Consequently, these past-life experiences may surface as purely physical conditions as well as psycho-emotional issues. In any case, the process of Integrated Imagery pays careful attention to the origination and release of those physical or somatic imprints associated with the behavioral and emotional manifestations.

Integrated Imagery is also well grounded in the principles and techniques of Carl Jung's analytical psychology. The concept of the collective unconscious and the archetypal roots that invariably underlie our psychological and karmic issues are always a consideration. The processing and guiding technique used in Integrated Imagery, in fact, has its basis in Jung's technique of active imagination. Jung used this as a way for clients to guide their own excursions into their unconscious process. We'll be using a form of Active Imagination throughout the course of the reflective and regression exercises that follow.

As you'll see in the next section, this approach also focuses on the presence of complexes that form the karmic patterns we carry through prior-life experience into the current life. The idea of the feeling-toned complex is also directly out of Jung's work. What we'll be working with throughout the rest of his book, however, is a more expansive model defining the formation and function of these complexes in our lives. This psychological model in many respects is a new and integrated way to look at human behavior and the effect of past experience on the present.

The *energetic chain of experience* (ECE) is another distinction of Integrated Imagery that deserves special attention. The energetic chain consists of the past-life, between-life, before-life, and perinatal states of consciousness that harbor the positive and negative memories of the past and the roots of the complexes we carry. It is throughout the energetic chain that we see complexes form and replay themselves. Consequently, in order to most effectively accentuate the positive and de-energize the negative, a regression technique must access as many of those antecedent experiences as necessary so as to leave no unresolved aspects of the complex. Each level of the ECE provides different insights and aspects to the themes and mission we carry into this life.

Although many regression techniques guide the subject not only through the significant incidents in the past life but also through the death experience, Integrated Imagery focuses special attention on the end-of-life experience. Supported by the work of Morris Netherton and Roger Woolger, the way we die in a past life dictates, to a great extent, the karmic patterns or complexes we carry forward. Consequently, Integrated Imagery calls for carefully processing the feelings, scripts (thoughts), physical sensations, and the activities surrounding those final moments in a given life. This is where the most insight may be gained regarding the impact of that life, and this is usually the period in the past life where reprocessing and resolution are most required. So, Integrated Imagery is a therapeutic technique that has proven to be most effective not only in awakening past lives but also in discharging and resolving the negative influences while activating and energizing the positive aspects of self.

In the Last Two Sections of This Book

The reflective exercises, the Active Imagination exercises, and the regression exercises you will experience are all based on the therapeutic regression model—Integrated Imagery. Take some time to reflect on the distinguishing characteristics of this model as you proceed with your own self-guided process. The real difference is that you will have my voice on the enclosed prerecorded CD guiding you through your energetic chain of experience. The transcript of the four Integrated Imagery sessions is in Appendix B. It would be a good idea to review those transcripts to familiarize yourself with the sessions you will experience.

Although you will have a slightly less personalized guidance through the process, remember that it is your unconscious mind which will play the greatest role in your awakening experience. So, rely on the fact that you will uncover exactly what you need to uncover and experience exactly what you need to experience on your own path to healing and growth.

Important Points in This Chapter

▶ Integrated Imagery is an experiential psychotherapeutic technique using hypnosis and altered states to explore prior experiences that are at the core of negative dysfunctional karmic patterns—to finish the unfinished business of the past.

▶ The technique makes use of traditional and some non-traditional therapeutic techniques.

▶ It also enables the exploration of positive karmic patterns and complexes.

▶ Integrated Imagery always considers the body/mind connection and the fact that complexes tend to manifest as physical symptoms as well as behavioral reactions.

▶ It is based on many of the principles and techniques out of the work of Carl G. Jung.

▶ It makes use of the expanded version of Jung's concept of "feeling-toned complexes."

▶ The technique calls for the exploration of the energetic chain of experience which includes not only past lives but between-life, before-life, perinatal, and biographical experiences.

▶ Integrated Imagery focuses on the death experience in past lives to provide insight as to the karmic patterns carried forward.

Section Two:
The Themes That We Carry

Now that we've explored the history of reincarnation thinking, the history of past-life regression therapy, the metaphysical system in the Cayce readings, and the laws of karma, let's look at just how the karmic patterns and themes (or complexes) form throughout the stages of our current and past lives.

We'll start to see how these different aspects that make up who we are in this world tend to interact with each other in sometimes complicated ways as they color the way we react to life's circumstances. And we'll see how they can be reflections of past-life experience. The actual case stories throughout these chapters should provide just a few examples of how our prior-life experiences can impact this life. Again, consider these chapters describing the formation and function of complexes as an important stage in your own awakening process. In each chapter be open to reflecting on your personal process and the insights that may present themselves.

The Purpose and Process of Life

Chapter 5

It is clear from our discussion of reincarnation thinking and the laws of karma that our personalities and that sense of "I" which we form in our biographical lives are influenced to one degree or another by before–life and prior–life experiences. From those prior lives we bring in or replay positive and negative characteristics, circumstances, and themes that become a part of who we are as individuals. These past–life themes or karmic complexes tend to show themselves or start to replay in biographical life right from the very beginning. Someone with a complex of abandonment, for example, might awaken at some point an in utero experience when mother thought about an abortion or felt resentment for being pregnant. In early childhood a parent might have died or abandoned the family by divorcing or just being emotionally disconnected.

These early biographical experiences provide opportunities for these karmic complexes to imprint in this life and start to manifest. With each successive biographical experience relating to a specific theme, the complex gathers more and more energy. The adult with the abandonment complex, for example, might look back time after time at an experience in life that in some way stimulated or reactivated that theme of abandonment. Examples of this theme might consist of having parents who were absent or emotionally disconnected or experiencing significant relationships that suddenly ended due to actions of others.

Before we look at the specific mechanism in the human psyche that forms a complex (whether in current or past lives), it will be helpful to look at the stages we all go through in this life from childhood and on through our adult years. By looking at the process of maturing from perinatal (in utero) beings through childhood and into our adult years, we can start to gain insight as to how these prior–life karmic complexes first appear, get activated, and imprint onto our current lives. In addition, we can start to see how the various developmental stages in life can have such a specific impact not only on the way we form and play out our positive themes but also how we may be burdened with the negative.

The First Order of Business

The first order of business in our biographical lives takes place during those formative years from conception to around age twenty. These years are the most formative because we are most dependent, especially in the beginning. We are highly receptive to learning survival and relational skills. This is when we have a heightened potential to initiate and develop those karmic skills, abilities, and ways of being that we bring into biographical life.

Once again, let's remember that this potential to develop positive patterns and complexes doesn't stop at age twenty. We will always have the opportunity to develop new complexes or to reactivate old ones. Free will also allows us to initiate and develop skills, abilities, and ways of being that have nothing to do with karma or past lives. At any time in life we have the opportunity to embark on activities that can develop into new patterns or complexes. The fact is that those first twenty years can be the most powerful in enabling us to optimize our karmic potential as well as any non-karmic patterns.

We all start life as helpless, little, dependent, and vulnerable beings with the mission of growing up into self-sustaining adults. This first order mission in our biographical lives involves learning how to survive in the world and how to relate to others in the process. So, it is in this process that we grow up physically as we develop emotional, psychological, and mental skills. All of these different aspects of our personality need to be tended to as we pursue this project of surviving and growing throughout the course of life.

Our modern culture and society can make this survival mission a little complicated. It's more than just growing or hunting food or finding a dry cave. Survival now has more to do with getting an education, finding appropriate work, making enough money to support ourselves and our families. It also requires developing more sophisticated relational skills that enable us to effectively collaborate with others while we create associations that support a sense of interconnection with those in the outside world. In simple terms, in our modern culture this is about developing skills, abilities, and ways of being in the world that allow us not just to survive but to thrive and continue this mission of growing or evolving—the mission of soul development.

Let's remember what the Cayce readings indicate: life is about being in the world to resolve and take advantage of our karmic complexes so that we may be free to pursue and fulfill our unique sense of soul purpose. This first order stage of life is when we start to see the first imprints of those karmic complexes.

The Transition Period

What happens next? In our 20s, 30s, and into our 40s, we start to exercise and practice that sense of "I" that formed in the first two decades of our lives. It is then that we start to put the work of the "first order" into action in our relationships, in our work, and in the process of living and making our way in the world. Erik Erikson, a noted developmental psychologist, defined this early adult period as a goal-directed search for purpose and meaning and a consolidation of identity. The identity is made up of all the positive and negative aspects of ourselves that constitute that sense of "I." The search indicates a transition period. Erikson goes on to say that this is a time of structure building and economic priorities and a time when achievement and the need for structure in our lives is a priority. This is when most of us finish our first level of education and training; we get our first serious jobs; we settle down, get married, and start to have families, and we make decisions that will cast a pattern for the next decades of our lives. The goal for the young adult is to strike out on his/her own to start to create a life that is truly separate from parents and family. In the beginning, especially, it is a time of experimentation concerning what we've formed and learned about ourselves in those first twenty years. It is a time to draw on and take advantage of all of our talents, skills, abilities, and chosen interests that will form a sense of direction or purpose in our lives. For most of us starting in our late teens and early twenties this is a time of really moving out into the world as independent, self-sustaining adults.

Bruce, who was raised in a family that put a high value on education and who supported his interest in science, finishes his training as a molecular biologist and embarks on a career in research and teaching. Connie, who always enjoyed taking care of her younger siblings and working with children, starts her career as an elementary school teacher with the dream of starting a family of her own.

In the Ideal World

Let's look for a moment at some of those survival and relational skills, abilities, and ways of being that support modern life. In the category of intellectual skills we can see that problem solving, curiosity, organization, and rational thinking are all aspects or skills associated with intellectual facility that can be cultivated throughout life. Being a good listener, having patience or compassion, and being a natural helper or mentor are also ways of being that can be developed to support this life mission of survival and personal growth. Artistic, athletic, and musical abilities can be cultivated from childhood and throughout our adult years—skills that can further enrich our lives. We can even look at self-confidence, a drive of determination, and a strong sense of responsibility as skills and ways of being that can be developed with the right experiences in life. The list goes on and on. The simple fact is as we develop any of these skills, abilities, and ways of being, they become for each of us aspects of ourselves that come together to form a sense of who we are as unique human beings—a sense of "I." Obviously, each of us will develop a set of skills and ways of being that is unique based on our life experience—and our past-life experiences. We also have the free will to focus on and develop new skills and abilities that are of interest. It's important to remember that any of these skills, abilities, or ways of being can be stimulated and developed at any time in our current lives. On top of this, through the process of Integrated Imagery we have the opportunity to awaken those aspects of ourselves that were perhaps unrecognized.

Before we go on, we need to address the issue of genetics and karma. Modern neuroscience has confirmed that there are specific inborn or inherited tendencies and predispositions that can form the seeds not only of our physical but behavioral differences. Obviously physical characteristics are inherited from our parents. Intellectual, aesthetic, athletic, musical, and artistic skills are some of the other predisposed tendencies or gifts which may be inherited. Let's not forget that just because we have inherited a specific ability, it does not mean we will develop that ability in this life. Circumstances and free will may prevent us from accessing, activating, or developing a given characteristic or way of being. Of course, the same applies to karmically inherited skills, abilities, and ways of being. The fact remains that whether or not these predisposed patterns or complexes are genetically or karmically based is of no real consequence. The implication is that in the before-life state—on a soul level—we chose to come into this life with the potential to develop those characteristics. In essence, the decision involved not only the karmic imprints but also the families, bodies, and genetic characteristics we are to deal with. The decision to take advantage of this opportunity then is dependent on the current life experience. And as the Cayce readings and the principles of karma indicate, the gift of free will can be a critical factor in developing any of these patterns or complexes.

The real question now is: What does it take to develop these positive and functional skills, abilities, and ways of being? In the ideal world, what is the course of life that will enable the activation and development of these positive patterns or complexes? How do we establish a sense of adequacy regarding any of these skills, abilities, or ways of being?

In the very beginning of this current life experience, we are the most dependent and vulnerable. It is during the early infant, toddler, and childhood years that we need to receive the most attention. We need to be fed, clothed, and sheltered. As important is the need to feel loved, protected, and nurtured. This need is initially fulfilled, for most of us, by parents and primary caregivers and eventually by our experience with siblings, family, and friends. In the ideal world all of these encounters with others are positive and assuring. We feel protected and safe. We feel nurtured and loved. And it is during these gestures and experiences from others that we first start to see how to react and interact with others in positive, caring, and constructive ways. Even when we have a difficult or traumatic experience in the course of life, it is the outside world that provides the support and protection we need to survive and learn.

Obviously, the need for protection and caring doesn't just start at the moment of birth. Research over the last twenty-five years has confirmed that even during the perinatal period from conception to birth (in utero), we are gathering experiences that impact our sense of being protected and nurtured. Loving, caring gestures from a pregnant mother or expectant father are actually experienced by the unborn fetus. Even the physical or emotional experiences of the mother tend to be experienced by the unborn child as their own. As mother starts to feel joy and elation with the thought of a newborn, so does the fetus experience those same feelings regarding the pending birth. And so, it is during this perinatal period that the seeds of our positive skills, abilities, and ways of being are planted. In fact, it follows that it is during the perinatal period these past-life complexes first implant or appear in the current life—in our physical and psycho-emotional bodies.

Let's go back to our biographical life experience and look at how we start to learn these survival and relational skills as we develop that unique sense of self—of "I"—in the ideal world. It's clear that the process of learning a skill, ability, or way of being starts with observing others display appropriate behavior. In the case of our early formative, vulnerable years, mommy and daddy (or significant caregivers) are the first teachers we have as they provide our basic needs for survival. Beyond those basic needs, the learning process continues as they help us to cultivate other ways of taking care of ourselves and relating to others. We gradually start to learn how to study, learn, play games, exercise our creative instincts, and play in groups. The whole process of learning centers on being instructed, observing, imitating, and exercising or practicing what we've learned. The critical factor in this learning process is that we approach the task with confidence and that we get positive reinforcement and encouragement. It is through these positive enlivening experiences and feedback that we not only learn these skills and behaviors but that we develop a sense of adequacy regarding our sense of mastery of a specific skill. This is a time when we first start to activate those karmic patterns and positive complexes.

Five-year-old Sammy with a natural karmic talent for music starts lessons under the suggestion of excited parents. His first teacher is positive and encouraging especially in the face of mistakes and wrong notes. It's not long before Sammy starts to get encouraging reactions from classmates and teachers at school. This is the beginning of a positive complex around the good musician. Eventually awards and accomplishments complete this process of confidence and adequacy regarding his ability as a musician and performer. Sammy has a positive complex that may or may not be genetically based but also has its karmic—past–life— roots. In any case, that complex was realized, exercised, and developed as a result of positive encouraging instruction and feedback from significant others in his life. As we've discussed, any skill and even ways of being in the world can be developed in the same way through the same set of encouraging life experiences. Behavior–based complexes like service to others and the good listener as well as skills like the good student and the athlete can all be developed and cultivated. So in the ideal world, all of life experience is positive, encouraging, and enlivening. All potentials are allowed their full opportunity to develop. And once we've started to develop those positive aspects of ourselves, we then go on into that transition period—in our late teens and twenties—to further develop and exercise those aspects. There is only one problem with this scenario: *Life is not ideal.* We don't always get the caring, protection, guidance, nurturing, or love that we need. We don't always experience skilled parents, caregivers, or mentors who bring a natural sense of encouragement to their interactions with others. We don't always have the opportunity to experience positive reinforcement in the face of our failures, nor do we always have interactions with the outside world that are life affirming. Life is not always fair. And as karma and Cayce indicate, we also bring these difficult circumstances and negative karmic patterns and complexes into our current lives from past lives—for the purpose of resolution and consequently soul growth.

In one form or another, these negative discouraging circumstances in life are experienced as threatening or traumatic. We can see that in many cases those who perpetrate the trauma don't do it consciously or purposefully. The fact remains that these traumatic experiences result in feelings of inadequacy around specific themes.

So, in this not–so–ideal world what happens? Just as in the case of those positive complexes we talked about earlier, negative complexes can be activated and energized from past lives or initiated in current life as a result of these not–so–ideal relationships and experiences. Criticism, abuse, neglect, and discouragement can all result in trauma that lies at the root of the negative complex.

Nancy, for example, grew up in those first twenty years with a critical father who was never encouraging, never expressed love, and often criticized her mother. A self-confidence complex resulted that kept her unable to pursue projects or relationships with any degree of success. A year of counseling with a skilled therapist didn't seem to help Nancy deal with this negative, self-defeating attitude she had about herself. It was in several Integrated Imagery sessions that we discovered the deeper roots to this karmic complex. We uncovered and processed several lives where she was repressed and criticized. One, in particular, held the most energy around her self-confidence complex. In that life she was a servant in a medieval household were she was made to feel inadequate about anything she did. Through continuitive karma she carried that pattern into this life. By redoing that life with a positive outcome and then exploring lives and biographical experiences regarding her positive complexes, Nancy was able to release this negative, self-defeating attitude she had about herself.

Brad had a mild learning disability that made reading difficult. Throughout his school years his negative intellectual complex was reinforced by damaging incident after incident until he finally dropped out of school. Until we started the regression work, he struggled with a sense of inadequacy regarding his ability to learn. In one past life he was the ruler of a small Chinese village where he prevented all of the young girls from pursuing any education. Retributive karma caused him to carry the repercussions of that life into his current life.

The case mentioned earlier in the Cayce readings is another perfect example of negative karmic complexes. The eleven-year-old bed-wetter came into this life with a negative complex that manifested as a physical issue. The warning to his parents was that his self-esteem could be damaged so much that he was in danger of not even attempting to pursue his soul purpose.

Again, these negative complexes can start to form at any time. But it is those early years when learning is more automatic and facile that they can more easily develop or be activated. In the next few chapters we'll look much more closely at how these complexes form and function in our current life. We'll also see how the same mechanism operates in past lives as well. Before we do, let's look at what happens next.

The Second Order of Business

In this second order of business that sense of "I" (with all the positive and negative complexes) and the way we exercise that "I" on a different dimension occur. Here we start to realize a different relationship with others and our environment. We start to become aware of the idea that "I" is both individual and indivisible from the outside world.

When does this second order work begin? For most of us it can start to come to prominence somewhere between our late thirties into our forties. This is when we might notice that there is more to life than we have experienced. It invariably brings up an awareness of the issue of life mission or soul purpose. It's important to remember that there is no set age when this second order awareness may come to the surface. It can occur at any time in life. In fact, we are likely to have inklings of it and the opportunity to engage this sense of mission even during our childhood (first order) years.

Let's look more specifically at how this works. Modern developmental psychology defines this second order mission as an opportunity for self-actualization. As we've said, this stage of life has more to do with the consideration of and integration of "I" with the outside world. The outside world now starts to represent more than just significant others, family, and peers. It becomes all that is outside of self—other peoples and cultures, the natural world, and even the world beyond the earthbound material world. The transpersonal or spiritual dimensions of consciousness come into consideration. A different relationship with the outside world starts to form with the sense that I am at the same time separate from and interconnected with all that is.

Many prominent psychologists including Carl Jung have addressed this stage of development. However, it was Abraham Maslow, a prominent psychologist, educator, and author, who emphasized and researched this stage as he defined its importance in human development. He describes self-actualization as " . . . the ongoing actualization of potentials, capacities, talents, as fulfillment of a mission (or call, fate, destiny, vocation), as a fuller knowledge of, and acceptance of, the person's own intrinsic nature, as an unceasing trend toward unity, integration or synergy within the person."[5]

Other psychologists have described and labeled this very stage at mid-life as integrated, generative, and value-oriented. Dr. Jenny Wade, a contemporary transpersonal psychologist, describes this stage most succinctly. In her model of the developmental stages throughout the life span she labels this second order stage as the authentic stage. She describes it as a time when:

> "Acts are simultaneously selfish and unselfish; the individual is equally concerned with his own personal growth and the welfare of all human beings. The authentic person pursues what

---

[5] Abraham Maslow, *Toward a Psychology of Being* (New York: Van Nostrand Reinhold Co., 1968), 25.

he desires, but never at the expense of others, and in such a manner that serves the greater good, not his own alone."[6]

The authentic self-actualizing individual is starting to accept the idea of being both individual and indivisible from the outside world. To be simultaneously selfish and unselfish, focused on personal growth and the welfare of all human beings as well as personal good and the greater good are all ways to express this authentic stage of development. It should be no surprise that this is also a perfect description of the sense of soul purpose emphasized in the Cayce readings.

Now, how does this look in the day-to-day life of the adult who is approaching the stage of self-actualization or becoming aware of his/her soul purpose?

This second order of business can be experienced and expressed in many different ways depending upon the individual. It may involve career changes, further education or training, or simply the pursuit of new and different activities. It may stimulate old (or new) creative interests (e.g., the arts, gardening, gourmet cooking, etc.) or altruistic pursuits. It will invariably bring one to a deeper awareness of his/her spiritual life. In any case, it will involve honoring one's authentic, perhaps newly discovered, sense of self ("I") but now with a different sensitivity and consideration for the outside world. In this sense if one allows his or her self to actively engage the work, it always brings new meaning to life.

Ann, for example, spent twenty years raising children and ten of those struggling in a contentious marriage. She worked at an unfulfilling job to provide a second income. At forty-eight, she ends the loveless relationship and pursues an MFA in creative writing—a passion she has only dabbled with in her adult life. She pursues this mission with the idea of expressing herself through her writing in a way that will be of benefit to the reader. Her Integrated Imagery sessions to explore her before-life experience perfectly validated and energized her deep-seated

---

[6]Jenny Wade, *Changes of Mind: A Holonomic Theory of the Evolution of Consciousness* (New York: State University of New York Press, 1996), 164.

desire to be a writer. It's not surprising that her past–life explorations uncovered several lifetimes where she had developed that talent as a writer.

Paul at forty-four sells his advertising agency—the great achievement in his life—to become a high school art teacher and to dedicate half his time to painting and selling his work. Larry takes an early retirement from a Fortune 500 company in his midfifties to fully invest himself in volunteer work to aid the homeless. In another example, Martha, who has been successful in medical sales most of her adult life, decides to seriously pursue her personal spiritual practice while finishing her doctorate in transpersonal psychology to become a spiritual counselor and teacher. In all of these cases, their before–life and past–life regressions uncovered, validated, and energized what they already had a sense of regarding their soul purpose in this second order stage of their lives.

It's important to remember, however, that this second order experience needn't involve such dramatic life changes. This stage may simply bring with it a change in one's way of being in the world or a change in attitude about one's life. Again it will involve a change in perspective or awareness from solely self–orientation and achievement to a sense of interconnectedness with others and the world.

In discussing this second order stage of life, there is an important qualifying fact to consider. For no one is there a certainty or a guarantee that s/he will be open to or move into this stage of development. As we'll discuss in later chapters, negative and even positive complexes may interfere with and disrupt these midlife opportunities for growth and expansion. These complexes may become distractions and complications that end up keeping one focused on the formation and self-indulgent preoccupation with the "I" as opposed to the work of also embracing the outside world.

There is another point for consideration, as we've mentioned. The first order work is never really finished. We are always in a process or have the opportunity to form new aspects of the "I"—new dimensions of who I am. New complexes or personal themes and behaviors, both positive and negative may form at any time. For this reason, it's better to think of the center of gravity in the first twenty plus years as being around "I" formation, the next twenty to thirty years around the application and expression of the "I," and from midlife on there is the opportunity to move on to a more self-actualized way of living.

By the same token, it is likely that at any time throughout the life span one may experience moments or times when s/he is open to those self-actualizing experiences that involve being both self- and other-focused. The altruistic teenager or twentysomething takes on a project with the sole purpose of service to others—not only for personal gain but also to make a contribution to a cause.

The emphasis in this chapter has been on these two most significant phases of life and the transition period between them. In the next chapters we'll focus on the formation and function of both positive and negative complexes as they develop in past lives and activate or transfer into current life.

Important Points in This Chapter

▶ In the first order of business—from the perinatal to the late teens or early twenties—we form the sense of "I."

▶ This is a time when our karmic complexes first imprint in our lives.

▶ In the transition period we exercise and practice that sense of "I."

▶ In the ideal world positive, reinforcing, and enlivening experiences enable us to develop a sense of adequacy regarding specific survival and relational skills and talents.

▶ Life is not ideal.

▶ We invariably experience negative or traumatic incidents in the course of life.

▶ In the second order of business around midlife, we have the opportunity to realize self-actualization when our sense of soul purpose can become even more pronounced.

▶ Negative complexes can interfere with this second order stage.

▶ Our first order business or the formation of that unique sense of "I" is never really finished.

▶ Integrated Imagery allows one to explore the prior-life antecedents of all three of these stages of biographical life.

An Exercise to Start to Explore
These Stages of Your Life

This exercise will help you to reflect more specifically on these three important stages in your life—the first order of business, the transition period, and the second order of business. The objective is to give you more insight regarding the process of your biographical life.

Prepare for the exercise:
- Retreat to your quiet place, have your journal and time line at hand.
- Review and reflect on what you've recorded so far on your time line.
- Use Track One on the CD to guide you through the progressive relaxation exercise.
- Set the intention of exploring these three stages of your life.

Start the exercise:
- Close your eyes and take several deep, relaxing breaths.
- Start the CD.
- Stop the CD when you've finished the progressive relaxation exercise.
- Reflect on these periods in your life.
  - Think about your first twenty years. What impact did those years have on your development as an adult? What were the most significant periods and experiences in those years? How did they affect your personality and the way you are as an adult?
  - Think about the time of your twenties, thirties, and forties—if you are that old. How did you experience this transition period? How did you make use of and exercise what you learned in those earlier years?
  - If you are in your late thirties, forties, or older, what is your experience of self-actualization as defined in previous chapters?
  - When you feel you've finished, just open your eyes, and come back fully refreshed and alert. Make any entries in your journal and your time line to record your insights.

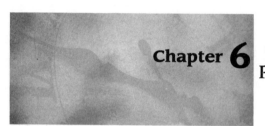

The Negative Complexes That Plague Our Lives

Chapter 6

If life—or our past lives—were ideal and all of our experiences were positive, encouraging, and enlivening, we would have nothing but positive complexes to draw on. Or if we negotiated each challenging or traumatic event to result in a positive outcome, positive complexes would also have the potential to form. But life is not ideal.

Invariably, each of us in the process of life and past lives will face experiences and circumstances that are traumatic, challenging, or emotionally shocking. Those experiences may be dramatic or subtle, persistent or episodic over a long period of time or in the short term. In any case, they can result in negative complexes that amount to unresolved aspects of ourselves which create dysfunction in our day-to-day biographical experience. An important point to remember is that each of us invariably brings negative as well as positive karmic patterns or complexes into this life in the process of soul growth.

Unlike the positive patterns that form out of enlivening incidents based on a sense of adequacy, the negative complex forms around a sense of inadequacy regarding ways of being, characteristics, skills, and behaviors. In this chapter in order to understand better how past-life experiences affect our current lives, we will talk about the structure of complexes and take a closer look at how they form. This applies to the formation of complexes whether in a prior life or in this one.

Carl Jung's Idea of the Complex

The term "complex" is pretty much a part of our common vocabulary. We've all heard of and probably referred to an inferiority complex. This is when an aspect of one's life seems less successful or inadequate. It was Carl Jung, a Swiss psychiatrist in the first half of the 1900s, who used the term complex as a part of his psychological model—analytical psychology. He talked about various complexes that reside in the personal unconscious mind of the individual and how they influence behavior or the way one experiences life events. Describing them as feeling-toned constellations in the unconscious, he goes on to say that they are:

> " . . . psychic fragments which have split off owing to traumatic influences or certain incompatible tendencies. . . . Complexes interfere with the intentions of the will and disturb the conscious performance; they produce disturbances of memory and blockages in the flow of associations; they appear and disappear according to their own laws . . . "[7]

In simple terms, they are like fragments or subpersonalities that form under different themes. And they come about as a result of personal experiences, starting in childhood, that point to unresolved problems. He emphasized the idea that these experiences were traumatic, either physically or emotionally. Consequently, his focus was primarily on the

---

[7]Carl Jung, *Collected Works of C.G. Jung, Volume 8* (Princeton, NJ: Princeton University Press, 1969), 121.

formation of negative complexes. Jung contended that each of us is predisposed to forming certain complexes because of tendencies within us that are unique to each of us. Although he never said it, the implication is that we are born with these unique predispositions. We can think of them as karmic patterns based in past lives and the collective nature of the human psyche. Jung did study Eastern philosophies, the spiritual dimensions of consciousness, and even astrology. Because of this and his emphasis on the collective nature of consciousness, he could be considered one of the modern pioneers in the field of transpersonal (spiritual) psychology even though he never directly addressed the issue of past lives or karma. In any case, Jung's idea of the complex suits us well as it relates to the karmic patterns we all must deal with in the course of life. Let's see why.

The Formation of Negative Complexes

Through my work with Integrated Imagery over the years, I have expanded on Jung's idea of complexes to define the mechanism by which these complexes form and how they function.

Before we go on, let's clarify the definition of "trauma." A traumatic experience can certainly be blatantly threatening. Being physically or sexually abused is a good example. Involvement in a life-threatening car accident can be as traumatic. These abusive, wounding, and threatening experiences we'll define as "lesion incidents." But trauma can be more subtle than that. As Jung puts it, an emotional shock or simply discouraging experiences can all be regarded as traumatic. The death of a parent or the emotional disconnection from a significant caregiver can have the same effect. Criticism or discouraging feedback from others can be enough of an emotional shock to form a lesion incident. Even self-assessed failure to succeed at an activity, like athletics or social interaction, can be considered traumatic and provide the foundation for a deep-rooted sense of inadequacy regarding that behavior.

These lesion incidents (or the traumatic experiences) can occur over a period of time or in a single experience. Whatever the case, they form around specific themes and generate *feelings, images, scripts, sensations* (F.I.S.S.) and *reactive behaviors* that give the complex a life of its own.

An Example of Negative Complex Formation

Let's take the case of Ben who entered Integrated Imagery therapy because he was concerned with difficulties in his intimate relationships with women. It became clear early in our sessions that he was struggling with an abandonment complex. At the time of his first session he was in a three-year relationship and engaged to be married. The relationship was not going well, and he was unjustifiably plagued with the fear that his fiancée would break off the engagement. Since high school Ben had been in two other long-term relationships (and engagements) with women who had broken them off.

If we look at Ben's childhood, we can see how this negative abandonment complex had formed and accumulated more and more energy. Ben was forty-three years old, born the youngest into a middle class family with three older siblings. He had a sister nine years older, a brother eleven years older, and another sister twelve years older. All three siblings were reported to be happily married with successful professional careers.

Ben's deceased mother had been a homemaker. His father was retired from a middle management job at a Fortune 500 company and living in a retirement community nearby. He described his mother as very nurturing and loving, but periodically depressed. Ben commented that "she really overworked herself taking care of the four of us and dealing with my father." It seems that his father had a very strong work ethic but tended to be emotionally withdrawn at home. He was a heavy drinker and could get abusive and hostile at the drop of a hat.

Ben remembers that between five and seven, his sister had severe asthma attacks which completely absorbed his mother's attention. Consequently, he was left with friends and neighbors for long periods of time.

Ben had prominent memories of his siblings during the period from nine- to eleven-years old. In session Ben reported, "By now they were all off to college and graduate school, and I was home alone with my parents." They all came home on holidays and weekends, but "every time they did, they would go out together at night." His sister to this day describes the pathetic look on his face when they would leave him home alone.

When Ben was fourteen, his mother was diagnosed with cancer. "The next few years were terrifying times for me in dealing with her sickness, and my father's drinking and depressive moods," Ben said. She finally died when Ben was sixteen, which put his father into an even deeper state of depression. His father's words continue to ring in his head, "crying isn't going to bring her back." So Ben stopped crying at sixteen. It wasn't long before Ben started drinking and became addicted to drugs. It wasn't until graduate school that a counselor helped him stop the addictive behavior, at least until he got into his first serious relationship in his twenties.

The loss of his mother was a trauma and a significant lesion incident that felt like abandonment. That loss alone could have formed the abandonment complex. But this was only the tip of the iceberg for Ben. His mother's periodic depression and preoccupation when he was a child also had its impact. His father's emotional withdrawal and hostility were consistent and sometimes subtle incidents of abandonment. Being left behind by his siblings and shuffled off to neighbors for long periods were all contributing factors.

All of these subtle and accumulating *lesion incidents* left Ben with *feelings* of fear, loneliness, inadequacy, and even rage. The *scripts* that formed, like "I'm all alone in the world"; "There's no one here for me"; and "It must be my fault," all followed him into adulthood. The redundant *images* of seeing loved ones leave, his father's rage, and the expression on his mother's face as she lay dying, all formed prominent memories. Even *physical sensations* manifesting as gastrointestinal symptoms, listlessness, and shortness of breath were reactions to these traumatizing incidents. All of these manifestations of his abandonment complex—the F.I.S.S.—are grounded in a deep sense of inadequacy about himself in relationship with significant others.

As Ben reached his twenties and started to engage in intimate relationships, his abandonment complex came into full bloom and gathered even more energy. His first engagement ended because his betrothed was emotionally disconnected and more interested in her work. His second girlfriend left him for another man. And his current girlfriend, who lived in another state, was starting to complain of Ben's clingy, needy, and controlling behavior. Suffice to say, Ben in his adult years continued to experience his abandonment complex which now seemed to have a life of its own.

It's worth mentioning that Ben, in other forms of psychotherapy, had touched on these earlier experiences and his sensitivity to being left behind. He even identified the negative thought patterns that persisted in his life. None of this helped him to resolve the abandonment complex that plagued his life. It wasn't until we did the past-life regression work through Integrated Imagery that all of the aspects of this negative complex came to the surface and started to lose energy.

One of his most prominent past-life experiences was that of a Bedouin elder. At the end of that life he was left in the wilderness to die of old age. All of the same *feelings, scripts and sensations* were a part of that life, but now with the *image* of his tribe and family moving off into the sunset. Here we see the past-life antecedents of Ben's abandonment complex. Again, we have good example of continuitive karma where this traumatic past-life experience continued to play out in a current life—not for punishment but simply to be resolved or de-energized.

After having uncovered this traumatic death experience in that life, I had Ben go back into that experience to do, say, and experience what he had not in that past life. In one incident he got up, ran after the tribe, and rejoined them to de-energize that abandonment experience. In another, he rested quietly and watched his tribe move on, knowing that this act was appropriate for that culture at the time and that he would rejoin them in another life. Through the reprocessing of this traumatic experience in the past, he was able to release himself from overpowering feelings of abandonment and the reactive behaviors that went with those feelings. Ben's relationship improved, and the last I heard he and his wife had had their second child.

Sarah's Problem with Authority

Sarah came into therapy with a real concern about her marriage. She hadn't been in therapy before and because of her curiosity about reincarnation she thought that past-life regression might give her some insight about her problems. As she reported, her husband was "very controlling, critical, and prone to having things his way." Soon enough it became clear that she was having similar problems in other aspects of her life. The problem seemed to center around situations where she or others were in positions of authority.

At work she took pride in her "take charge" leadership skills. The problem arose, however, when she would overreact to someone, especially superiors who questioned her approach or her decisions. She was also accused of resenting and routinely defying those in higher positions. Obviously, this didn't sit well in the corporate organizational setting, and Sarah found herself moving from one job to another. She moved from being controlling and overbearing in her relationships to feeling victimized and unfairly treated by others who exerted some degree of authority. Sarah has an authority complex.

As we delved into Sarah's history, the biographical roots of this complex soon became clear. Her father was extremely controlling and abusive. He dominated her mother, and her older brother was an even more prominent target for abuse and criticism. Her father's mantra was: "I rule this family and don't even think about questioning that." Although Sarah experienced very little of her father's aggressive behavior, she saw her mother and brother constantly victimized, controlled, and criticized. As we continued to work with this authority theme, she started to get in touch with *feelings* of fear, resentment, and disempowerment when faced with circumstances where she wasn't in control or when her ideas were not fully accepted. The old *scripts*, "My life is out of control" and "what I feel and think is worthless," seemed to be ever present. She even reported *physical sensations* of nausea and body tension while sitting through a business meeting. Sarah was carrying the feelings, scripts, sensations, and even the images that formed in her childhood experience with her father. Those many lesion incidents where she experienced or observed his overbearing behavior formed the root of her authority complex. And now, her work life and her marriage were suffering because of this complex.

After identifying her biographical history and the dynamics with her father, we started the process of Integrated Imagery. Her past-life regression work revealed obvious antecedents of this sensitivity and issue with authority. In a Greek life, an early biblical life, and a Native American life, she was imprisoned by rival factions, abused, and executed.

Those lives energized her experience in this life as she grew up in a household where she felt imprisoned and threatened. In another life she rallied a rebellion to overthrow a cruel and dictatorial ruling family in a small province in Renaissance Italy. That life ended again with incarceration and death after challenging the authority figures of the time. Sarah was in the throes of continuitive karma as she carried the theme of persecution by authority into this life. In all of these lives she experienced that same feelings, scripts, and sensations that she experienced in this life. Only the images were different.

One life was particularly interesting. In an Asian life in the early nineteenth century she rose to power as a beneficent tribal leader totally focused on the well-being of her people. This life provided another karmic pattern; this time she carried forward a positive complex of the compassionate leader and a deeper insight and skill as to what it takes to be a good leader. Sarah certainly displayed the characteristics of a good leader or authority figure. What she had to deal with in this life, however, was the negative karma that was unresolved from the past.

By awakening those past-life memories and reprocessing the traumatic experiences, Sarah was finally able to de-energize the negative complex that plagued her life. In the Greek, biblical, and Native American lives, I guided her to imagine escaping her captors and living a fulfilling life. In the Renaissance life she imagined successfully overthrowing the ruling family and freeing her people. We also revisited that Asian life when she had first developed that positive complex of the compassionate leader. In that regression I had her focus on the positive feelings, images, scripts, and sensations that resulted from her accomplishments in that life—all in the process of accentuating the positive while de-energizing the negative. It was also important to explore some of the other aspects of her energetic chain of experience. The insights from her between-life experiences helped her to see the implications of those prior lives and the karmic patterns she continued into this life. In her before life it was clear that she made the decision to bring to this life not only the soul purpose of the compassionate leader but also the negative complexes to be resolved. Her marriage relationship started to improve as her tendency to feel criticized and controlled was desensitized. And her authority issues at work were gradually resolved.

The previous examples of negative complex themes are just a starting point. What is most important in identifying and dealing with negative complexes is the actual structure of the complex. This structure includes the *feelings, images, scripts, sensations (F.I.S.S.)* and the lesion incidences that surface during the regression experience and in the course of our biographical lives. Equally important are the reactive behaviors that the complex carries.

Some Examples of the Themes of Negative Complexes

Unworthiness	*Rejection*
Self-esteem/Self-worth	*Self-confidence*
Superiority	*Inferiority*
Narcissistic	*Self-deprecating*
Dependency	*Independence*
Abandonment	*Betrayal*
Outsider	*Risk taker*
Caretaker	*Rescuer*
Pleaser	*Savior*
Defeatist	*Achiever*
Victim	*Authority*
Criticism	*Control/Power*
Stupidity	*Vulnerability*
Chaos	*Confusion*

The Reactive Behaviors of Negative Complexes

In addition to the associated F.I.S.S., negative complexes also carry specific behaviors that are essentially reactions to the lesion incidences or traumatic experiences of the past. If we are threatened or are in danger, we might fight back in rage or flee with fear. If an incident causes negative feelings like guilt, jealousy, disgust, or shame (just to name a few), we might depress or shut down those feelings. If we are in danger of losing something or someone, we might cling or try to control the situation. If we are neglected or criticized, we might become self-absorbed and narcissistic. Because of the body/mind connection, those reactive behaviors also carry with them physical or somatic reactions that obviously affect our bodies. For example, fear or anger will raise blood pressure and trigger the adrenal glands. Depression can result in tiredness and lethargy.

In all of these cases, these reactive behaviors are defense mechanisms that result from those threatening or hurtful "lesion" experiences of the past, whether perceived or real. These behavioral and somatic reactions all become a part of the mechanism of the complex. And along with the feelings, images, scripts, and sensations, they are the defensive reactions that surface in the course of life. They affect the way we experience life. The problem is that they take on a life of their own, and they normally surface when we really don't need them. These reactive behaviors also surface in three ways: (1) conditioned reactions/somatic imprints, (2) reactive behaviors/somatic reactions, and (3) repetitive reactions.

Take the case of Ben with his abandonment complex. He engages life with an unconscious fear of being abandoned by loved ones. Consequently, the *conditioned behavior* associated with this complex causes him to consistently and unconsciously display behavior that is clingy and over accommodating. His first girlfriend, who was required to travel for her job, was a perfect trigger for his complex. Ben would continuously inquire about her whereabouts and consistently put aside his responsibilities to be with her. These behavior patterns became a part of how Ben presented himself to the world and to his intimate partners. It wasn't surprising that his second and third betrothed both complained of the same behavior—or defense mechanism.

The *somatic imprint* connected with his clingy behavior comes across as a need to be in physical contact as much as possible. When that's not possible, he starts to feel tense and anxious. In this way he is unconsciously literally trying to hold onto these women out of a fear of loss. His *conditioned behavior and somatic imprint* become a part of the way Ben meets the world. They unconsciously and consistently affect his behavior and his physical body, regardless of the circumstances.

His *acute reactive behavior* took a different form. When his first girlfriend had to go off on a business trip for example, Ben would initially get aggressive and demanding before settling into a state of depression. In this way his acute reactive demanding behavior was an unconscious effort to prevent her from leaving and the depression defended him against feeling all of the pain of being left behind, alone, and abandoned. The *somatic reaction* would get to the point of raising his blood pressure and creating a physical numbness that could be unbearable. The *acute reactive behavior and somatic reactions* surfaced episodically when a life experience acted as a trigger. Again, these reactions followed him throughout all of his intimate relationships and interfered with each of them. Ben was clearly overreacting to a common life experience which is exactly the way Jung described the clue that a complex was activated. In this way Ben was bringing sensitivity from the past into the present in a dysfunctional manner. In the first two relationships the abandonment theme created problems that eventually undermined the relationship. We can see that these defensive reactive behaviors and physical reactions were the same experienced by the Bedouin elder left behind by his tribe.

Ben also displayed another defensive reaction to his fear of abandonment. In his first serious relationship he started to use drugs and alcohol again in a repetitive, addictive fashion even when the relationship was going well. Underlying this *repetitive behavior*, the compulsion to use drugs, was the fear of abandonment. The substance abuse managed to at least temporarily dull those feelings, images, scripts, and sensations that were so painful. This was the unconscious driving force that first started in his late teens with his mother's death and his father's withdrawal into depression. Here it surfaced again as a way of repressing that pervasive fear of rejection and being left behind.

In the case of Sarah we can see other examples of the way these reactive behaviors surface. With a complex around authority, her *conditioned behavior* actually caused her to take on a demeanor of authority. Her posture and even her physical gestures indicated one with self-confidence and leadership skills, which in effect was a defensive reaction against being controlled. Underlying that persona of self-confidence was a constant vigilance for being challenged or questioned. This even plays through physically out of a *somatic imprint* as she experiences a certain level of body tension and anxiety as soon as she engages subordinates or enters her place of work.

When Sarah's authority or leadership approach is challenged, her *acute reactive* behavior is triggered, and she routinely becomes antagonistic and defiant. In these cases she is often overreacting to a common life experience as she feels unjustifiably criticized, controlled, and persecuted—just like her experience in her family and her past lives. Her *somatic reaction* causes her to take an aggressive in–your–face posture that prepares her to fight for her position. This antagonistic behavior and aggressive posture are exactly the approaches she took when challenging those autocratic authority figures in a past life. It was this defensive reaction in the past that became a defensive reactive carryover in this life. Of course, the same consequences followed in both as she ends up being persecuted for her actions.

In the case of her *repetitive reactions*, Sarah doesn't struggle with any classic physical addictions like alcohol, drugs, or food. Instead, her addictive repetitive behavior amounts to a compulsive drive to stay organized and to micromanage the activities of her subordinates. In this way, she can unconsciously guard against the possibility of having her own authority called into question.

The process of doing Integrated Imagery through the energetic chain of experience, in most cases, reveals the antecedents of these behavioral reactions and defenses that are carried forward from the past-life experiences. All three of these reactive behaviors (conditioned behavior, acute reactions and repetitive reactions) resurface again to guard or defend against the lesion incidents of the past. In the words of Carl Jung, the problem is that they cause us to over- or underreact to a common life experience.

So far we've talked in detail about the negative complex themes of abandonment and authority. But negative complexes come in all varieties. Power, inferiority, savior, betrayal, and control are just a few of the themes that form into complexes. All of these possibilities boil down to an inadequate sense of self or some aspect of self.

Negative Complexes Come in Other Forms

Negative complexes can also organize around specific skills or abilities. The case of Eric is a prime example. Eric is a professional writer and the chair of creative writing at a major university in California. In spite of his professional accomplishments as a teacher with eight published books, all of which have been recognized in the field of non-fiction, Eric has a negative complex around the skill of writing. During his high school and undergraduate years, his writing was criticized by two teachers for whom he had very high regard. Although their criticism was constructive and intended to enable him to continue to develop what seemed to be an inborn talent for writing fiction, it had the opposite effect. He became discouraged and apprehensive about his ability to tell a fictional story in words. It didn't prevent him from pursuing this passion for writing. It did, however, continue to get in the way of his dream and soul purpose of becoming a novelist.

Several past lives revealed the root cause of his sensitivity and complex—this block to his passion for fiction writing. In one medieval life he was a storyteller who traveled the English countryside spinning fictional stories meant to be inspiring to the common people of the time. That life ended in persecution when he was accused of attempting to stir a rebellion among the downtrodden serfs in a small village. He died repeating the phrase, "I'll never tell another story." In another life as an Asian female, a passion for pursuing the intellectual life was squelched when that young maiden was not allowed to learn how to read or write. A perinatal (in utero) memory came through in Eric's Integrated Imagery work when he heard his parents, who were both business professionals, casually discussing a concern that their child would grow up with a desire to be an artist. These past experiences were enough to imprint sensitivity to fiction writing that was inadvertently reinforced by those two teachers in his school years. With his very specific complex came feelings, images, scripts, sensations, and the reactive behaviors that are parts of the negative complex. Reinforced in his past-life, perinatal, and biographical experience, his complex came out full blown to unconsciously undermine what for him was an important aspect of his soul purpose in this life. Eric's writer's complex continued to stifle this passion until we explored the deeper roots of this complex. In reliving those past lives, that traveling minstrel was allowed to escape his captors and continue his mission of storytelling. That Asian maiden was educated and allowed to live the life of a teacher and writer. After this work, Eric's last two novels have received wide acclaim.

We see from the case of Eric that a negative complex can form around a skill, ability, or a specific behavioral characteristic. The talent or a simple interest in athletics, art, music, or parenting can all be stifled by a negative complex. Any behavioral characteristic can end up being the theme for a complex. Even something as simple as the skill for driving a car can be affected by the formation of a complex—especially if one has experienced a trauma or threatening experience while driving.

The Physical Manifestation of a Complex

In the three examples of Ben, Sarah, and Eric, we see a full blown replay of the complex with all of its aspects surfacing at one point or another. But negative complexes don't always surface in such a full blown fashion.

If we go back to the witch dunker in the Cayce readings, we can see a good example of a purely physical manifestation of a complex formed in a past life. In this case the aspect or the somatic imprint of wetting is the only way this complex from the past appears in this life. What drives this manifestation is retributive karma in that there is a reversal from the dunker/perpetrator to the self-wetter/victim. But only the physical aspect is carried forward. This can happen in many forms when we talk about the physical manifestations of a negative complex. Severe muscular problems, respiratory problems, or chronic migraines are just a few of the ways the experiences out of the past may surface in this life. Invariably when we awaken the past-life roots of these physical symptoms in this life, what we reveal is the full story including the incidents, the feelings, the scripts, and the images that formed the complex in the first place. In this awakening process the whole story usually needs to be brought to awareness in order to fully understand the implications of these antecedent experiences and to de-energize their impact on this life. The witch dunker in the past-life sought out with vengeance innocent children whom he thought were possessed by evil spirits. That dunking experience for them was obviously traumatic and most likely damaging to their self-esteem. According to the Cayce reading, retributive karma was in effect. That witch dunker was now dunking himself in the process of undoing that traumatic deed of the past.

If I had had the opportunity to work with that eleven-year-old bed-wetter using Integrated Imagery, the objective would be to revisit that witch-dunker life and redo the experience. One way to de-energize the act of the perpetrator might be to imagine not terrorizing those children with dunking. Another way might be to visit the souls of those children in the between-life state and ask for forgiveness. In any case, it would involve undoing the wrongful act that was done.

Just as in the case of the witch dunker, a complex may surface through a single aspect. For example, a feeling, an image, a script, or a single reactive (defensive) behavior may provide the clue to a karmic complex. That simple aspect of the complex can have the same disruptive effect on the current life of the holder. A chronic depression, a pervasive feeling of loneliness, a physical manifestation, a repetitive compulsive behavior, or a repeating negative self-defeating thought might be the only clue that a complex from the past is surfacing. For this reason, it is important to explore the experiences in the entire energetic chain of experience in order to fully understand and address the entire structure and the prior-life roots of a complex.

A Note about Biographical History

In my experience using the technique of Integrated Imagery, there have been cases where there was no biographical history that contributed to the formation of a negative complex. The case of a thirty-two-year-old woman is a prime example. She came into therapy displaying all of the signs of post-traumatic stress disorder, an eating disorder, and the strong possibility of having been sexually abused as a child. As we carefully and thoroughly explored her childhood history, it became clear that sexual trauma was not a part of her current life experience. Nor were there any other current life experiences that would explain the symptoms she was struggling with. The sexual abuse at the root of these symptoms was only experienced in a past life. By uncovering and processing that past-life story, her symptoms were relieved, and she was able to move on in this life without the F.I.S.S. and reactive behaviors from that past.

Important Points in This Chapter

▶ Negative complexes are constellations of energy that form around themes relating to skills, talents, values, and ways of being.
▶ These themes carry an obvious sense of inadequacy.
▶ These negative complexes form as a result of "lesion incidents" that reinforce the theme.
▶ Associated with these lesion incidents are feelings, images, scripts, and physical sensations (F.I.S.S.).
▶ Although negative complexes are likely to form at any time in life, they are more likely to form in one or more past lives.
▶ As the core of the negative complex forms around the lesion incidents and the F.I.S.S., three reactive behaviors and somatic reactions develop that serve to defend against the negative aspects of the complex.
▶ The three reactive behaviors in the negative complex are (1) conditioned behavior, (2) acute reactions, and (3) repetitive reactions.
▶ The complex eventually takes on a life of its own as it affects one's experience of life.
▶ These negative complexes can and often do interfere with the holder's pursuit of soul purpose.

An Exercise to Further Define Your Negative Complexes

In this exercise you'll continue to explore your biographical current life history in the process of uncovering potential negative complexes. Go back to your autobiographical time line and start to reflect on those challenging, difficult, and traumatic experiences that may be a clue to your own negative complexes.

- On your time line in each ten year period, notate incidents or periods in your life that were particularly challenging, difficult, or traumatic.
- What memories or images are most prominent and repetitive in your life—in your recollections, dreams, and self-guided imagery?

- Who were the people involved? What was happening? How were you feeling?
- What reactions did you display in these incidents?
- Have these experiences been repeated later on in your life?
- Most important, what are the scripts or persistent thoughts coming out of these experiences that have stayed with you to this day?
- Just reflect on these questions without the need to draw any conclusions or define any specific theme or complex.

Chapter 7

The Formation and Function of Positive Complexes

In the last chapter we went into detail regarding the formation and function of negative complexes and the karmic history behind them. In this chapter we'll focus on positive complexes and their implication on the sense of soul purpose that is unique to each of us. As mentioned earlier, most approaches to past–life regression therapy involve concentrating on the negative karmic aspects of life. In fact, most people come into therapy because of some problem in their lives. Obviously, it is important to deal with these problems and the negative complexes that surface. Equally important, however, are the positive complexes or the karmic gifts that we carry into this life, which also have their roots in past–life experience. These are the aspects, themes, or karmic patterns that make up our unique personalities and invariably have much to do with soul purpose.

A Positive Complex Associated With a Skill

The case of John is a good example of the formation and past-life karmic history of a positive complex associated with a skill. John had a positive complex of the good musician. He was born into a family where both parents were accomplished professional musicians. Because he seems to express an early interest in playing an instrument, his father starts him with music lessons at eight years old. Both his mother and father provide nothing but support and encouragement during those first few years. Gradually, John starts to be recognized by family, friends, and classmates as a good musician. Time after time he is singled out as talented and eventually he starts to win awards and gains even further recognition in his high school years. What's more, John manages to develop his talent not only as a classical performer but also as an accomplished rock-and-roll and jazz musician. Associated with all of these *enlivening experiences* regarding his musical talent are *feelings* of excitement, joy, and pride when he practices or performs. *Images* of these enlivening experiences in performance and practice stay in his memory. He can remember scenes of an audience applauding after a concert and the proud expression on his father's face. When he thinks of performing, he automatically hears the *scripts* of recognition and praise from his parents and others that all reinforce his confidence. Even *physical sensations* of excitement and emotion surface whenever he thinks of his passion for music. It is these *feelings, images, scripts, and sensations* (F.I.S.S.) surrounding the many positive enlivening experiences that form the core of his positive complex. We can see that eventually with enough emotional, visual, mental, and even physical energy accumulating around a specific theme, the complex takes on a life of its own. When John hears another performer play, his good–musician complex stimulates for him a different kind of experience. He feels it differently from others in his emotions and even in his body. In his day–to–day life he is unusually attuned to sounds and music around him. When he is asked to play or when he starts a practice session, those feelings, images, scripts, and sensations come to the surface to enliven his experience and provide a sense of confidence and adequacy. The karmic theme of the good musician comes into this life as a kind of subpersonality that becomes a part of who John is in this life.

In one past life, John was a Native American medicine man who used his handcrafted flute to awaken the spirits of the deceased. In Renaissance Italy and medieval England he was also an accomplished musician who received a great deal of recognition. The seeds of this talent in this life were clearly planted in those past lives. And they carried the same feelings, images, scripts and sensations that formed the basis of this complex. It was by revisiting these past lives that John realized how important music was to him in this life. It didn't move him to change careers, but it did rekindle his interest and the creative inspiration that comes with playing music.

There was another benefit to his regression work. John initially came into therapy to deal with problems he was having at work. He complained of depression; he was unmotivated and was starting to receive poor performance reviews. The creative stimulation that resulted from revisiting these lives and reinvigorating his good-musician complex soon carried over into his work life. His depression lifted, and he started to find new ways to invest this creative energy in his career.

A Positive Complex Regarding Ways of Being

We've seen in John's case how a positive complex can form around a specific skill, talent, or ability. The good student, the artist, the athlete are just some of the examples. The good listener, the organizer, and the leader are also part of another set of skills that can be significant complexes and aspect of one's personality. As important are the complexes that can form around values and ways of being. Sally is a good example.

Sally came into therapy struggling with depression and hopelessness. In the initial session she reported that her live-in partner of five years had recently ended the relationship and moved out. She was despondent and terrified that she could not make it on her own—financially or emotionally. What was interesting was that her early life demonstrated a history of self-sufficiency.

From an early age, Sally was encouraged to do things for herself. At first she was nurtured and taken care of by her parents and older siblings. But even as a toddler she was encouraged and praised when she displayed behavior that indicated she could do things for herself. When she fed herself, went to the potty alone, or asked for something she wanted, she experienced positive, reinforcing feedback from those around her. She started to gather more and more enlivening experiences around the theme of self-sufficiency. When she failed, she wasn't punished but was corrected and given the chance to try again. As she was appreciated, validated, understood, and given more opportunities to do things for herself, more and more positive energy accumulated around this theme. Gradually she expanded her base of experience into other behaviors that related to self-sufficiency. This self-sufficiency complex became more of an attitude or way of being that incorporated many different behaviors and skills. At the center of this feeling of adequacy about self-sufficiency were those enlivening incidences that formed her self-sufficiency complex. Constellating around this core of experiences are the *feelings, images, scripts,* and *sensations (F.I.S.S.)* that keep the complex alive and active.

If we look at the karmic or past-life roots of Sally's complex of independence and self-sufficiency, we can see where this started. In doing Integrated Imagery with Sally we discovered that in one life she was accidently separated from her primitive Inuit tribe and found herself in the wilderness alone. To survive she had to fend for herself without the support of others. In a Roman life, her husband was forced to leave her alone with five small children as he went off to fight the wars of the time. She again had to make her own way with no help from her family or community. In both of these past lives she died with a real feeling of adequacy and satisfaction. These and several other lives formed a positive complex around this theme of self-sufficiency.

Simply reminding Sally of her ability in this life to take care of herself didn't seem to be enough to pull her out of depression and fear. It was by revisiting and reprocessing those positive past lives that she was finally able to bring herself to her feet and create a new life for herself.

The case of Ann is another good example of the formation of a positive complex relating to a way of being—this time it was a helper complex. She grew up in a family which modeled this behavior. When anyone connected with her parents was in need of help, her parents were there. They were always recognized as caring people who would rise to any occasion if needed. Ann consequently grew up feeling good about being of service and supporting those in her life who were less fortunate or who were going through difficult times. Ann herself was consistently recognized and praised for her interest and competency in helping others. This helper complex soon became an important part of who Ann was in the world and how she was perceived by others.

Ann came into therapy not because of some debilitating occurrence in her life but to explore the idea of soul purpose. At forty-five years old she realized that there was something more to life than her work as an administrative assistant for an insurance executive. She had certainly been exercising her helper complex in her work and home life, but she realized that something was missing.

Several Integrated Imagery sessions focused on soul purpose illuminated for Ann the past-life roots of this helper complex. In a Native American life she was a tribal leader driven by the need to care for and protect his people from the invading European forces. In an earlier life in primitive Africa she was assigned the responsibility of caring for the children in her village. In both of these cases Ann exercised on a soul level continuative karma as she carried this positive complex forward into this life. But there is another aspect of her regression work that shed another light on the past-life antecedents of the helper complex. In one life Ann went back to a time where she was the ruler of a small village in medieval times. In that life she acted as a tyrant, took advantage of her followers, and worked only to her own benefit. In the between-life and before-life states it was confirmed that through continuitive karma she brought this positive helper complex forward from those admirable lives as a caretaker of others into this life to balance the negative energy of the self-oriented leader. And for Ann, the process of Integrated Imagery was important in validating and stimulating her soul purpose in this life—to be of service to others as she drew on her positive helper complex.

Within two years, Ann found a new direction in her life when she finished her Master's degree and became an elementary school teacher driven by this need to be of service. Not surprising, she spent much of her free time volunteering at her church and donating part of her earnings to worthy causes. In the case of Ann, this helper complex formed into a real sense of soul purpose that provides meaning in her life to this day.

Some Examples of Positive Themes or Complexes

Self-confidence	*Self-sufficiency*
Self-survival	*Integrity*
Helper/Caregiver	*Responsibility*
Creativity/Imaginative	*Cooperation*
Organization	*Risk taking*
Initiative/Proactivity	*Generosity*
Friendship/Relational	*Sense of humor*
Forgiving/Understanding	*Nature/Animal lover*
Empathetic/Understanding	*Logical/Practical*
Leadership	*Encouraging/Supportive*
Curiosity	*Problem solver*

Skills: Intellectual, Artistic, Musical, Athletic, Verbal, Written, Mechanical, etc.

Before we go on, let's remember one important point: both positive and negative complexes most likely have a past-life history. In other words, they were initially formed and reinforced in prior lives. We must not forget, however, that in our current biographical life we also have the ability to start the formation of a completely new positive (or negative) complex at any time.

Positive Complexes in the Therapeutic Process

Obviously, Integrated Imagery is a therapeutic technique that allows one to deal with and de-energize those negative or dysfunctional aspects that plague us. Equally important, as we've seen in these cases, it enables the deeper exploration of those positive aspects that we carry into this life. There are three ways this exploration of positive complexes can be of benefit:

- To explore, enliven, and perhaps reactivate positive karmic complexes that were already recognized in this life.

- To awaken and invigorate those positive complexes which are important aspects of one's soul purpose.
- To uncover complexes that may have been unrecognized or dormant in the course of one's biographical life.

In process of doing Integrated Imagery to explore these positive complexes, it's important to focus on the feelings, images, scripts, and sensations that form the core of any complex. It's also important to be aware of the way these complexes surface or get triggered in the normal course of life.

The Reactive Behaviors of the Complex

Just as in the case of negative complexes, positive complexes carry with them reactive behaviors and somatic reactions that play an important role in our biographical lives. As the core of a positive complex starts to develop around enlivening incidences and as more and more emotional, mental, visual, and physical energy (F.I.S.S.) accumulate around the theme, the same three specific sets of behaviors start to form just as with negative complexes. There is one important difference regarding the purpose of these reactive experiences. With negative complexes they are the defense mechanisms that were protective devices against the trauma of the lesion incidences that formed the complex. In the case of positive complexes they are actually behavioral and physical reactions that serve to preserve the enlivening incidences and the positive skills, talents, and ways of being that are associated with the complex.

These reactive behaviors affect our behavior in the course of life. They essentially color the way we experience and react to life circumstances. Aside from enabling us to make use of the positive aspects of the complex, they keep the complex alive and reinforce its further development. They allow us to continue to add positive experiences (enlivening incidents) and energy to the core of the complex.

Conditioned Behavior and the Somatic Imprint

In the case of *conditioned behavior* we have a positive reactive behavior that consistently affects the way we experience life and the way we meet the world through the persona. John's good–musician complex consistently and most times unconsciously causes him to be sensitive not only to music but to the common sounds in his day–to–day experience. Without even realizing it, he is more emotionally and mentally attuned than most people to tones, rhythms, pitch, and frequencies because of his accomplishment as a musician. On the physical side, John also tends to have a heightened physical reaction to sounds. This *somatic imprint* from the good–musician complex may cause him to have a positive physical reaction to the routine noise and music of the world.

Ann with her helper complex also meets the world in a different way. In her case, her drive to be of service and her sense of adequacy associated with that characteristic are reflected in her persona. Ann's very demeanor is that of being there for others. Even when the need is not obvious or necessary, she is consistently attuned to helping, always offering positive encouraging advice, always displaying empathy and a sense of readiness. Her somatic imprint is even reflected in her physical appearance with opened arms and a gentle comforting touch.

The self–sufficiency complex that Sally has developed surfaces in consistent and subtle behavior. Consequently, she is more attuned to doing things for herself without asking or expecting help from others.

So with conditioned behavior and the associated somatic imprint we can see the consistent effect of the particular positive complex. The theme becomes an obvious part of the holder's personality. The attributes of the good listener, the artist, the compassionate caregiver, the athlete, and others become a part of how that individual meets the world and experiences the process of life. In the case of this type of reactive behavior, very little stimulation is needed from the outside world.

Acute Behavior and the Somatic Reaction

Acute behaviors and the *somatic reactions* operate in a slightly different way. Again, they both help to preserve the positive characteristics of the complex, allowing the holder to make us of complex when appropriate. They also provide the opportunity to continue to add positive reinforcing energy to the core of the complex. The difference with acute behaviors is that they require an external trigger or circumstance to stimulate the attributes and the F.I.S.S. of the complex. John may be overly sensitive and open to the sounds and music around him, but when a colleague asks him to play a job or take part in a jam session, his musician complex is triggered. He immediately feels a heightened sense of confidence and excitement with the opportunity to exercise his talent. He will invariably experience a physical—somatic reaction—as well, possibly resulting in an elevated pulse or blood pressure. This kind of acute reaction allows John to rise to the occasion and to draw on the talent he has developed and brought into this life.

Ann goes through a similar experience when someone asks her for help or an emergency presents itself. Her helper complex kicks in full force allowing her to rise to the occasion and to be of service. It is then that the attributes and learned skills of this positive complex are brought into action and even further developed. Her enlivening memories, her feelings, images, scripts, and even physical sensations are all activated with a sense of adequacy. Her somatic reaction in these circumstances can serve to raise her adrenaline levels or even activate in her system neurological networks that cause her to be more attuned to the expressions of others.

In the case of Sally with the self-sufficiency complex mentioned earlier, she may display a consistent demeanor of self-confidence and optimism. It is when circumstances arise requiring her to take action and fend for herself that the acute reaction comes into play to activate her complex.

Repetitive Reactions

The third set of reactive behaviors—the *repetitive reactions*—provide another vehicle for a positive complex to surface. Like the conditioned reactions, they may be unconscious and more consistent in their appearance. And like the acute reactions, they may respond to a specific life circumstance or trigger. What is unique to this set of behaviors is that it takes the form of more compulsive behaviors or actions which surface to activate the complex.

The good-student or intellect complex may manifest as an extra attentiveness to learning, observing, or taking in information on a consistent basis through conditioned behavior. When stimulated by an opportunity to gain more information from a book or lecture, the acute reaction comes into play to stimulate the positive learning complex—to allow one to rise to the occasion. It is the repetitive behavior, however, that may keep the holder almost compulsively engaged in an activity that draws on the complex.

John's repetitive reaction around the good musician may manifest in an insatiable or even compulsive drive to practice his instrument or listen to music. If he doesn't get enough practice time, he's likely to feel uncomfortable and out of sorts without even knowing why. Sally's self-sufficiency complex may push her into a kind of compulsive activity of organizing her time and her life so that she's always on top of things and never has to ask for help. Ann may find herself putting aside all other activities as she tirelessly volunteers her time and money to her charities. This repetitive drive may be subtle or more pronounced. Whatever the case there will be some degree of this persistent, almost addictive behavior associated with each complex.

As with the other reactive behaviors, there is also a physical reaction that is stimulated along with the repetitive behavior. In this case the physical sensation can be in the form of discomfort or anxiety that is put to rest by enacting the behavior. John's physical anxiety is relieved when he puts in practice time. Sally's discomfort is addressed only when she feels organized and prepared.

In the case of positive complexes, these three reactive behaviors (conditioned, acute, and repetitive) and their associated somatic reactions allow us to draw on the accumulated characteristics of the complex. They clearly color the way we experience life and how we play out these positive themes or aspects of ourselves.

In the process of Integrated Imagery with clients, it can be important to be aware of how these positive complexes tend to surface in one's life as well as in past lives. In the course of the following reflective exercises regarding your biographical life and the regression sessions in the next section, be aware of these reactive behaviors and the somatic reactions as clues to your own positive complexes.

Important Points in This Chapter

▶ Positive complexes are constellations of energy that form around themes relating to skills, talents, values, and ways of being.

▶ These themes carry an obvious sense of adequacy.

▶ These positive complexes form as a result of enlivening incidents that reinforce the theme.

▶ Associated with these enlivening incidences are feelings, images, scripts, and sensations—F.I.S.S.

▶ Although positive complexes may start to form at any time in life, they are more likely born in one or more past lives.

▶ As the core of the complex forms around the enlivening incidents and the F.I.S.S., three reactive behaviors and the associated somatic reactions develop that serve to preserve and perpetuate the complex.

▶ The reactive behaviors are (1) conditioned behavior, (2) acute reactions, and (3) repetitive behaviors.

▶ The complex eventually takes on a life of its own as it affects one's experience of life.

▶ One or more of the positive complexes tend to come together to constitute the holder's unique sense of soul purpose.

An Exercise to Take Stock of the Positive Complexes in Your Life

• Go back to the autobiographical time line you started in the last chapter. Take as much time as you need to reflect on the positive experiences in each ten–year period of time.

• Start your reflection by relaxing with a few deep breaths and letting go of any tension in your body. Take as much time as you need to relax into a quiet, safe reflective feeling.

• Think about your positive skills, abilities, characteristics, and ways of being. Make a list.

- On your time line notate any positive experiences you remember that relate to any of these attributes.
- What was happening? Who else was involved? How were you feeling? Make more detailed notes in you journal.
- Reflect on the relationships in your life at the time—your parents, siblings, friends, other family members, teachers. How were they supportive and encouraging?
- Most important, what are the scripts or persistent thoughts coming out of these experiences that have stayed with you to this day?
- At this point, reflect on how some or all of these experiences were connected.
- Take your time—don't rush. Focus on one ten-year time period at a time.

Just reflect on these experiences without the need to draw any conclusions or define any specific theme or complex.

The Interactive Dynamics of Complexes

Chapter 8

We've spent the last two chapters talking about how positive and negative complexes form and function in our lives. It's time to start to look at how these distinct aspects of our personality relate to each other, not only in our daily lives but also in our prior-life experiences. How do they add to and detract from each other? And how do they affect this process of awakening and the pursuit of soul purpose? It'll also be helpful at the end of this chapter to take a closer look at how complexes surface and how they are triggered in our relationships and the circumstances of life. How do they enhance and disrupt the course of our lives?

As we go on talking about the effects of complexes on human behavior, continue to reflect on your own life. Keep your autobiographical time line at hand. Take reflective time to deepen further your understanding of how your past affects your current experience.

A Word about Soul Purpose

Positive complexes, remember, are grounded in a sense of adequacy relating to skills, abilities, values, and ways of being. That sense of adequacy associated with these themes is reinforced by feelings, images, scripts, and sensations. The characteristics of the complex are preserved by the associated reactive behaviors that form. These positive karmic patterns, then, are brought into this life to be used and possibly to become vehicles for one's pursuit of soul purpose.

On the other hand, negative complexes, based on a feeling of inadequacy, bring with them defensive reactive behaviors. These are protective reactions that formed as a result of lesion incidents or traumatic, threatening, or wounding experiences. These defensive behaviors helped us to survive in the past, but they bring with them an unresolved history that maintains a life of its own. We've survived these incidents, but we carry with us the residue of those experiences.

The executed, abused, betrayed, or abandoned character who dies with fear and resentment energizes the karmic complex in this life. The powerless leader who dies with guilt and shame after having let his followers down carries those same feelings forward through continuitive karma—all because of unfinished or unresolved experiences of the past.

These unresolved karmic patterns carry forward in another way. Through retributive karma the persecutor in a past life becomes the persecuted in this life. Again, this negative complex is experienced in this life not for punishment but to balance or resolve that negative energy—all in the process of soul-level learning.

So, one part of the mission in this life or any life is to resolve the unresolved—to finish the unfinished business of the past. Until we do, those negative karmic patterns/complexes will tend to disrupt our lives. As Carl Jung would say, they will have us until we manage to de-energize them enough to where we have them. Even the Cayce readings confirm that one aspect of purpose in this life is to address and balance that negative energy out of the past as we pursue our unique mission of soul purpose. Let's not forget that both positive and negative complexes tend to have karmic past-life roots. But they can form in our biographical lives with no past-life history.

As noted in Chapter Two, there is another even more prominent aspect of soul purpose, and that is to realize a very specific and unique mission in this life. Whatever the theme is, that mission results in a deeper understanding of one's relationship to the Divine and gives insight into the purposefulness of all life. It opens one to an expanded awareness, and there is a critical dimension regarding service to others. On top of that, the realization and pursuit of one's soul purpose provide a feeling of great joy. Again, this is not about what we do but how we engage life—a way of being that is unique to each of us. To be sensitive to the have-nots of the world, to be an innovator, to synthesize and blend, and to be a spiritual leader are just a few of the themes that may constitute soul purpose.

The previously mentioned humanistic and transpersonal psychologists all addressed this idea of soul purpose in one way or another. Carl Jung refers to the process of individuation. Others use the term self-actualization. Abraham Maslow's definition fits perfectly with this idea of soul purpose that Cayce talked about. He describes self-actualization as " . . . the ongoing actualization of potentials, capacities, talents, as fulfillment of a mission . . . as an unceasing trend toward unity, integration or synergy within the person."[8]

So we bring into this life these potentials, capacities, and talents or positive complexes to fulfill a mission. This mission, in one way or another, involves service to others and results in a sense of unity, integration, and synergy as well as an acceptance of one's intrinsic nature. It is the negative karmic complexes that invariably interact with those positive aspects that can cause the problem.

So, let's go on and look at how all of these experiences and dimensions of ourselves from the past come together to affect our current life experience. How do positive and negative complexes interact with each other in disruptive and helpful ways, especially as they relate to soul purpose?

---

[8] Abraham Maslow, *Toward a Psychology of Being* (New York: Van Nostrand Reinhold Co., 1968), 25.

The Ego Matrix Is the Container

From all that we've talked about, it's easy to see that none of us is a one-dimensional being. We all have many aspects of ourselves that come together to make up who we are—that sense of "I." And even the most conscious of us is bound to carry aspects that are unrealized, unrecognized, or only partially formed. In other words, especially if we consider the idea of karma, these are aspects or potentials that reside in the unconscious.

This process of awakening then—the purpose of this book—is about uncovering all of these various aspects or positive and negative complexes. In addition, it involves accentuating the positive and de-energizing the negative as we find and pursue our unique sense of purpose.

The container for these many aspects of self we'll call the ego matrix. Modern psychology has other titles for this sense of self or "I." It is a matrix because it is very much an array of parts or complexes that have the potential and the tendency to interact with each other. This is where our conscious and unconscious complexes reside, and this is where they start to interact with each other.

How the Complexes Interact

There are three ways that these active—conscious or unconscious—aspects of ourselves living in the ego matrix interact with each other. There are ways in which complexes join forces in productive and not so productive ways. For example, like complexes—positive with positive and negative with negative—can interact with each other to either enliven the positive or exacerbate these negative aspects of the holder. On top of that, negative complexes can take over and make use of positive complexes in disruptive ways. Finally, the reverse can happen where positive complexes actually take over aspects of negative complexes.

Let's start with the case of *like complexes interacting with like complexes.* We see an enlivening effect when two positive complexes come together and interact with each other in the course of our lives. In the case of John's good-musician complex, if he also has a healthy complex regarding service to others, we may see him using that musical talent and skill in conjunction with his need to help others. A positive self-worth complex, interacting with the good musician could serve to drive him even more into a career in music as he draws on the positive energy from both.

Cayce's witch dunker reading provides another example for the combination of two karmic complexes. In this case, the nine-year-old child brings in a positive karmic complex as an artist from one past life and that of a spiritual leader from another. In this life they have the potential of joining forces—enlivening each other—and, in fact, forming that child's soul purpose of providing spiritual guidance to others through the visual arts.

The reverse effect can happen when two negative complexes join forces to become even more disruptive in one's life. Sarah's authority complex could be even more accentuated if she also has a betrayal complex. Her sensitivity toward betrayal can easily compound her issue with authority figures. Now the active script becomes: people in authority will betray and persecute me. Ben's inherent fear of being abandoned would be even more accentuated if he also lives with a diminished feeling of self-worth.

In the case of *negative complexes taking over positive*, we have more good examples from the cases we've talked about. This is when these negative patterns actually make use of the positive complexes or specific aspects of these complexes as defense mechanisms to subdue the negative and painful experiences harbored in the core of the complex.

Because of his abandonment complex, Ben was fearful of being left behind by his significant others. But he also had a positive complex regarding his intellect. When he started to feel the fear of abandonment surface, he tended to intellectualize the relationship and the dynamics in the relationship. He used his intellect to cling to his partner. In other words, the intellect became another defense mechanism to squelch the pain and fear of abandonment.

Sarah had developed a skill (positive complex) as a leader in a past life. That positive complex, brought in through continuitive karma, allowed her to make use of that skill in this life, but her negative authority complex made use of her ability as a defense mechanism to advance to leadership positions to protect her from feeling dominated and controlled by authority figures. Obviously, it backfired on her until she started to understand how those complexes interacted. By understanding the dynamics of these complexes—and processing them through Integrated Imagery—Sarah was able to move on with her life and become a very effective leader and a successful business woman.

The classic case is that of the care*giver* with a healthy positive karmic complex regarding being of service to others. If we couple this admirable pattern with a deeper feeling of inadequacy or negative self-worth, that care-*giver* becomes the care-*taker*. Now, those positive gestures of being the helper are undertaken mainly to deal with those deeper feelings of inadequacy about self. The agenda and the script then becomes: if I am there for everyone, then I will be worth something in the world. Instead of giving simply because one can, this individual ends up giving out of fear—to get something. The person becomes the *taker* not the *giver*.

So in these cases, a complex involving self-worth, betrayal, criticism, or any focal point of inadequacy can take over a positive complex associated with a skill, ability, value, or way of being in order to protect the holder.

These examples have shown how some of the positive attributes of a complex can be distorted into dysfunctional behavior. But there is another way that this can work. John, the good musician, could be struggling with a self-worth complex. That very deep feeling of inadequacy could very well take hold of his good musician and drive him to practice and succeed—all to help deal with the discomfort of his negative complex. In this case, we can see a positive outcome that could be a very productive way of reacting to the presence of a negative self-worth complex. In this way a *positive complex is making use of a negative complex* to further accentuate the positive. That is if John's commitment to practice and success is kept in check. If not, John's drive can turn into an obsessive-compulsive pattern of behavior that could have productive results (success in music) while only exacerbating the pain and suffering that holds that negative complex together. This is a case where John can alleviate the reaction to that negative complex. Until he deals directly, however, with his inadequacy, he will continue to struggle one way or another with an issue of self-worth.

A Word of Caution

Don't be overwhelmed trying to figure out how these interactive dynamics of the complex might play out in your personal case. It can be a tricky exercise to figure out how all of these positive and negative aspects of the various complexes work for you. Rest assured that in the next section you'll have the opportunity to explore these potentially complicated dynamics with more clarity. Through the regression, reflection, and Active Imagination exercises you'll be able to start to put your own puzzle together.

Before you go on, take some time to reflect on what you know about yourself. Think about the complexes you're aware of so far and how they might interact with each other. Go back to your autobiographical time line and journal the insights that come to you.

How the Complexes in the Ego Matrix Surface

In the last two chapters which described the formation of positive and negative complexes, we saw how both carry with them specific reactive behaviors and somatic reactions along with the feelings, images, scripts, and sensations. In the case of positive complexes, they help us draw on or make use of the attributes of the complex. With negative complexes, they are also helpful devices, but this time in a defensive way to protect us from the replay of those threatening and traumatic incidents that formed the complex in the first place. In this way they can help us to survive the trials and tribulations of life. Coming into this life with a betrayal complex gives one the skills and sensitivity to protect oneself from those who might betray. The problem, of course, is that these reactive behaviors which are sensitivities and protective devices tend to surface when we don't really need them. They have a life of their own. In Carl Jung's terms, they cause us to over- or underreact to a common life experience. As we've seen, they form around unfinished business from the past that disrupt our lives. Again, these are the unresolved experiences not only of past lives but also of our biographical lives.

We've looked at a number of examples of how this works. Obviously, having access to these skills, talents, values, and ways of being is a good thing. These are the positive karmic patterns that energize our lives and make us unique individuals. But what about the negative stuff? What's good about having these negative karmic patterns?

In one way or another Carl Jung, the transpersonal psychologists, most of the metaphysical systems, and certainly the Edgar Cayce readings all confirm that an important aspect of our purpose in this life is to deal with and resolve these negative karmic patterns. Consequently, it's good that these unresolved aspects of ourselves surface so that we may deal with them and finish the unfinished business of the past, thereby getting to the point, as Jung puts it, that we have the complex and the complex doesn't have us. In order to do this soul-purpose work most effectively, we need to be aware of and awaken both the positive and the negative patterns that we come into this life with. And most important, we need to understand how they might affect our pursuit of soul purpose.

The technique of Integrated Imagery is a proven and effective tool that we'll use in the last section to help awaken these past-life experiences. A helpful starting point in this self-discovery process is to look at how these karmic complexes have been surfacing and expressing themselves in your life to date. How have your experiences in this life, in relationships, and the activities of life triggered both your positive and negative complexes? That has been the objective of the exercises so far. To help in your reflective process, let's take a look at three ways that complexes get activated and play out in life experience.

The Magnetic Energy of Complexes

Jung states that complexes seem to have a magnetic energy that draws to us affiliations and associations that tend to play out the complex. In other words, unconsciously without intention we can rely on the fact that people and circumstances will automatically appear in our lives that trigger both our positive and negative complexes.

Ben, once again, is a perfect example of how this works. In at least his first two serious relationships he seemed to draw women who were emotionally disengaged and ultimately uncommitted to the relationship. The first was preoccupied with her job, and the second, with other men. In both cases, Ben chose or magnetized partners who were bound to abandon him.

Sarah, with an authority complex, ended up being attracted to and marrying someone who was very controlling and prone to having things his way. Here again, her complex magnetized one who would consistently trigger her sensitivity to those in authority—like a husband or a superior.

Fortunately, the same magnetic attraction works with positive complexes. Take Ann's helper complex from Chapter Seven. She had actually grown up in an extended family and a neighborhood where those around her seemed to have an inordinate tendency for helplessness. There always seemed to be someone who was coming to her and her parents with problems. Her parents were also good role models for Ann as they were always ready to pitch in when someone was in need. Ann always seemed to have the opportunity to exercise her helper complex without going out of her way to find someone in need. Those in need were magnetized to Ann and her family.

Another Implication

If we look carefully at our lives, we can all see situations and relationships that we have unintentionally created for ourselves. There are situations that have a tendency to trigger our complexes by unconsciously magnetizing people and circumstances that activate these karmic patterns.

If we look closely at the cases of Ben, Sarah, and John, there is another implication. They all came into families that were destined to set up and activate their unique complexes. The implication is that they were predestined to form these patterns. In doing Integrated Imagery with all three of them, it became clear that their choice of parents and even life circumstances, in fact, were made even prior to conception in the before–life state. The Cayce readings, karmic laws, and certainly the past–life regression literature all indicate that we do actually select future life circumstances that will develop and activate our karmic complexes. We even have the option of choosing our astrological birth chart that supports our karmic mission. So the magnetizing effect of the complexes in many cases is set up before life begins.

In the next section, when you start the Integrated Imagery exercises, we'll use the before–life aspect of the energetic chain of experience to help you gain insight as to your mission and karmic patterns—as to the decisions you made before coming into this life. For now, it's important to remember that this tendency to magnetize affiliations and associations is not about predestination. What it means is that we can be sure that the opportunities will be there for us to exercise our free will as we travel through life on our soul purpose paths.

Complexes Get Projected

The classic definition of a *projection* involves unconsciously attributing to others some characteristic, emotion, trait, or value that we hold ourselves. For example, in the case of a positive complex—conscious or unconscious—we would tend to admire others who have the same characteristics. There is another way that this projection mechanism works, especially in the case of negative complexes. In this case, we end up projecting behaviors onto others that are identical or similar to the lesion incidents that initially created our negative complexes. That unconscious memory which resulted in trauma and the associated behavior is imagined to be happening again, bringing with it the defensive reactive behaviors that were formed.

Ben's mother abandoned him by dying. His father emotionally abandoned him with his drinking and criticism. The Bedouin elders abandoned him in a past life by leaving him to die alone. By simply telling him that she can't meet him Sunday night because she has to study for an exam, his current girlfriend triggers for Ben that deep–rooted sense of abandonment which has nothing to do with the current situation. He is projecting onto her those abandoning characters of the past. Ben essentially is hallucinating that she is leaving him behind even though she has no intention of doing so. With this current experience come the defensive reactions. He gets depressed, clingy, and controlling. Ben is overreacting to a common life experience because of the projection of his abandonment complex. His Integrated Imagery sessions that allowed him to revisit, rescript, redo, and de-energize his complex were critical in eliminating his sensitivity and tendency to unjustifiably project these experiences.

Sarah projects onto her boss some unreasonable act of controlling her when he simply asks her for her weekly expense report. She gets aggressive and argumentative. Eric's negative complex regarding his fiction writing is triggered when a student asks him to explain what the message was in one of his stories. He gets defensive, withdrawn, and despondent. In all of these cases the projection puts one into a place of overreacting to a common life experience (triggering the negative complex) by imagining that they are re-experiencing a lesion incident.

The same type of reaction can happen in the case of a positive complex, but with different results. In this case, the positive enlivening incidents are projected onto another's behavior or a situation, and the complex of adequacy is triggered into action. It's important to remember that the projection is an exaggeration of the circumstances and not necessarily based on the reality of the situation.

Ann's helper complex will tend to be activated when a friend asks for help. In this case her acute reactive behavior (along with her somatic reaction) is triggered as the complex surfaces. But, in the case of a projection, that same reactive behavior may be stimulated when there is only Ann's perception of a need by someone. Here she unconsciously assumes that her best friend is in need of help when she casually mentions that she forgot to pick up an item at the supermarket. She, without thinking, springs into her helper mode.

How We Unconsciously Induce a Complex

The third type of trigger for our complexes gets a bit more complicated. And especially in the case of negative complexes, it can be more troublesome to deal with. In this type—the *induced trigger*—the holder of the complex unconsciously displays behavior that causes others to behave in ways that will trigger the complex. The holder may also display behavior that sets up entire situations which act as a trigger.

In Ben's third session he related a recent experience with his current girlfriend that explains how this works. Two weeks before the session he mentioned to her that he had some minor reservations about planning their marriage. Within a few days she started to withdraw and not respond to his phone calls. She was obviously questioning his commitment to the relationship and moving into a protective mode herself. Ben came into the session depressed, reporting that it was happening again; his girlfriend was abandoning him. It didn't take much to get him to see how he had set up the entire situation that understandably forced her to withdraw. Ben had unconsciously induced her to abandon him.

What was interesting and insightful in Ben's case was a regression that we did at the end of that session. During a past life in the sixteenth century he had left his wife and three children behind to selfishly pursue fame and fortune. That negative karmic pattern, this time as the one who abandoned others, was the antecedent for his inducing action. As he reflected on other situations in this relationship and the others, Ben started to see how prevalent this behavior was in the way he engaged in relationships.

Sarah also displayed this type of inducing behavior in certain situations. In her case, she would tend to get argumentative in the normal course of her encounters with her superiors. In these situations they were often forced to take charge and lay down the law, thus triggering her authority complex.

To This Point

We've looked at the ways that complexes can relate to or interact with each other in the ego matrix. And we've covered how all complexes may be triggered in the normal course of life. It's important to understand that this process of awakening is not just an intellectual exercise. The real insight as to how your positive and negative complexes operate and how they affect your soul purpose will come out of the Integrated Imagery exercises in the last several chapters. Just rely on your unconscious mind to reveal the memories that will not only provide this insight but also enable the process of finishing that unfinished business.

Some Important Points in This Chapter

▶ The ego matrix is that part of the human psyche that harbors all of the many complexes that come together to make up who we are—the sense of "I."

▶ The complexes in the ego matrix affect how we meet our experience in life.

▶ The complexes invariably interact with each other in three ways.

▶ Like complexes interact with like complexes

▶ Negative complexes can take over positive complexes.

▶ Positive complexes can take over negative complexes.

▶ All complexes or combinations of complexes can be triggered or brought into action in three ways.

▶ Complexes seem to have a magnetic attraction that draws to us people and situations that trigger the complex.

▶ Aspects of the complex may be projected onto the behavior of people and onto situations that trigger the complex.

▶ Complexes can unconsciously force us to display behaviors that can induce others to behave in ways that trigger our complexes.

▶ Complexes, aspects of complexes, and the interactive dynamics of complexes tend to have their roots or beginnings in prior life experiences.

▶ Integrated Imagery is an effective and proven way to awaken these prior-life experiences and to accentuate the positive as we de-energize the negative.

▶ In this process of awakening we have the opportunity to optimize our pursuit of soul purpose.

An Exercise to Reflect on the Interactive Dynamics of Your Complexes

• Go back to your autobiographical time line and reflect on your life experience based on what you've just read.

• Think about the formation and function of your complexes.

• Think about those positive aspects of your personality and whether they might qualify as positive complexes.

- Think about any negative aspects in the same way.
- How have these positive and negative aspects interacted and surfaced in your life? Make any notations on your time line when these incidences have occurred.
- Have you seemed to draw people and circumstances that have triggered positive and negative reactions in your life?
- Have you noticed situations where you might have projected or induced specific behaviors in others?
- Reflect on people that you admire. What is it about their lives, their abilities, or their ways of being that you admire?
- Reflect on people that you are uncomfortable with or dislike. What is it about their behavior that triggers this feeling or impression?

Take some time to notate and journal any thoughts that come to you before going on to the next chapter.

Section Three:
Exploring Your Biographical Life—
An Introspective Process

Now we are about to embark on a very different—and much more personal—approach to past lives and soul purpose. Recall that in Section One we explored the history and principles of reincarnation and karma. We saw how these ideas about karma and soul purpose were brought into a modern context especially through the intuitively derived spiritual psychology of Edgar Cayce. We also traced the history of past-life regression which eventually became a psychotherapeutic approach paralleling the development of modern psychology. And in Chapter Four I explained the technique of Integrated Imagery that was developed through my clinical experience over the last twenty plus years.

Section Two examined how positive and negative themes can form as a result of life experiences—past and present. Special focus was placed on how these themes or complexes interact with each other in helpful and disruptive ways. These interactions are especially relevant to the pursuit of one's soul purpose. The exercises in these chapters have been an important starting point in your self-discovery process.

In the next two chapters in this section you'll be guided through exercises to enable you to further define the positive and negative themes or complexes that affect your current life. In this process you'll make use of Track One on the enclosed prerecorded CD to guide you into a feeling of relaxation as you reflect on the experiences in your current life. This will be a journey of clarifying and expanding on what you already know about yourself and one of new discoveries. Relax and enjoy the trip.

Chapter **9**

Taking Stock of the Positive Themes and Complexes in Your Life

In this chapter, you'll focus on defining and clarifying positive themes or complexes that color this life and how they may be a part of your personal life mission or soul purpose. As you take part in the exercises in this chapter (and the next), keep in mind the central objective of this personal experiential journey: to uncover and accentuate the positive while de-energizing the negative themes or complexes—all in the process of clarifying and pursuing your soul purpose.

Recall from Section Two that positive complexes are formed as a result of positive experiences in your past. Those positive enlivening incidents carry with them feelings, images, scripts (thoughts), and physical sensations which accumulate under specific themes. These complexes are also associated with specific behaviors that help you to draw on or make use of these themes later in life.

The story of Mary is a prime example. She grew up with two parents who continually reinforced the ideas that she think for herself and be independent. They not only set an example but also acknowledged and encouraged her creative thinking and independent behavior. As an adult Mary is a self-confident, self-motivated independent woman. She has a positive self-confidence complex which will serve her throughout life.

John has a positive complex around a specific skill. He started music lessons at an early age with his parents and several good music teachers. Into his late teens, he received acknowledgment and positive reinforcement for his musical ability. To this day John carries a positive complex regarding his musical talent.

As indicated in these examples, each complex is based on a feeling of adequacy regarding a specific characteristic or theme. And it's helpful to remember that positive complexes needn't take years of positive enlivening incidences to develop. They can form with just a few positive reinforcing experiences in your past history. By looking back into your current life experiences, you can start to define positive complexes that influence your life today.

As you proceed, keep these important points in mind:

- Positive complexes are not only formed in your current life; more likely than not, they were formed and experienced in your karmic or past-life history.
- Positive complexes tend to be vehicles for one's personal sense of soul purpose.
- It is possible during these exercises that you'll experience negative memories, behaviors, feelings, and reactions. If this occurs, for the time being journal your insights and put those negative feelings and reactions aside as you refocus on the positive.
- During this experiential journey, you'll discover new insights regarding your positive complexes and possibly even uncover positive themes you haven't been aware of. Keep an open mind—and enjoy the journey.

Exercise One: Positive Complexes in Your Autobiographical Time Line

In this next exercise, go back to the autobiographical time line that you started to prepare in the Introduction. This is a time to further define the formation and function of those positive complexes.

Prepare for the exercise:
- Once again find a quiet and comfortable place where you can relax and reflect on your life—a place where you will not be disturbed.
- Have at hand your autobiographical time line, journal, and any drawing materials you might like.
- Set the intention of clarifying the most prominent complexes. Allow yourself to be open to new insights about these aspects of yourself and how they play out in your life.
- Relax by taking several deep breaths to let go of any tension you may be holding.

Start the exercise:

As you proceed with this exercise, it's best to focus on one ten–year period at a time. Take as much time as you need to reflect on your life and the positive experiences in each ten–year period before going on to the next one.
- Review your time line and all the journal entries you've made so far.
- Carefully reflect on the following questions:
  1) What skills, talents, activities, and behaviors do you feel good about?
     - Reflect first on those aspects of yourself that you feel positive about or feel a sense of adequacy.
     - Reflect on your accomplishments and/or times that you were recognized/acknowledged for an accomplishment.
     - How did these attributes and characteristics develop?
     - Do they seem natural and inborn or did you have to work at learning and developing them?
     - Make a list of these characteristics.
  2) What aspects of your character do you feel good about?

- Think about your values, attitudes, morals, philosophy of life, and ways of being. Examples might be honesty, service to others, independence.
- Reflect on how these characteristics play out in relationships, at work, in your leisure time, in the way you live your life.
- Think about your emotional, mental, physical, and spiritual well-being.
- How did these characteristics develop? As you reflect on your time line, think about when these characteristics appeared in your life and how they continued to play out.
- Make a list of these characteristics in your journal.

3) What are the feelings, images, scripts, and physical sensations associated with these characteristics and aspects of you?

4) Reflect on all of these positive aspects and how they were influenced by experiences and the people in your life.
- Think about your parents, siblings, and family members.
- Think about your friends, peers, teachers, and mentors.
- Think about famous or historical people you have studied and respect. What is it about them that impresses you? How have they influenced you? How are you like them?

5) Finally, when you feel you've completed this exploration of your positive complexes, journal all of your insights before moving on.

Exercise Two: The Positive Aspects of Who You Are

This exercise will help you to define and zero in more clearly on the positive aspects of your personality—those positive complexes formed in this life known as your biographical life. We'll use the technique of Active Imagination to access memories and insights harbored in your unconscious mind.

To start the Active Imagination experience you'll go through a progressive relaxation exercise to slowly relax the body and allow yourself to focus on the insights that come to you. Track One on the enclosed CD is a recording of my voice to guide you through this progressive relaxation. When you're ready to proceed, play the CD until you hear me say, "now you can proceed with your intention to explore and gain insight

about your themes or complexes." At that point, stop the CD and proceed with your active imagination. The script for this progressive relaxation exercise is also in the following paragraphs. It will be helpful to
read through the script before you start in order to familiarize yourself
with the suggestions to relax.

There is a second option to starting this exercise—especially if you
don't have a CD player. Simply memorize the script and talk yourself
through the relaxation.

A third option is to prepare a tape of the guiding script using your
own voice or that of someone else reading the script. The transcript of
the progressive relaxation exercise is in Appendix B.

Active Imagination

In the process of Active Imagination, the first step is to *set an intention*.
This could be an intention to explore a dream or an experience in a
dream. It could be a reflection on an experience in the past that stimulated a feeling or thought. In the case of this exercise, the intention will
be to explore and gain insight about your positive complexes and the
history of their formation in your biographical life. More specifically
you can focus on the function and history of a particular positive complex. In any case, expect to gain an even deeper insight into your positive
complexes; one that is beyond what you discovered in the last exercise.

The next step is to *suspend all judgment and analysis* during the exercise
and let the feelings, images, thoughts or scripts, and physical sensations
surface as you proceed. Feel free to directly engage anything that surfaces
by *entering into a dialogue* with it. Ask questions and listen for a response.
As you reflect on your life, when specific characters appear, directly engage them in a dialogue. Again ask questions and wait for a response.

Prepare for the exercise:
- When you're ready, find a quiet and comfortable place where you can
  relax and reflect on your life–a place where you will not be disturbed.
- Have your autobiographical time line, journal, and any drawing
  materials with you. Take a moment to reflect on what you've discovered so far about your positive themes and complexes.

- Set the intention to focus on your positive characteristics and aspects or to focus on a particular positive characteristic.
- As you concentrate on the intention, allow yourself to experience the feelings, images, scripts (words, thoughts, phrases), and physical sensations that surface.
- Focus on what impressions come up as you open yourself to whatever your unconscious wants you to see and experience:
  o Suspend any judgment or analysis for the time being.
  o Switch off your analytical mind.
  o Just let the impressions appear.
- You can remember everything that occurs to you during this exploration.
- Take as much time as you need to process any impressions that come to you.

Start the exercise:
- Close your eyes and take several deep, relaxing breaths.
- Start Track One on the enclosed CD, or listen to your taped version, or talk yourself through the following progressive relaxation exercise and allow yourself to move into a relaxed feeling of peace and calm.
- When you hear the statement, "Now you can proceed with your intention to explore and gain insight about your themes or complexes," stop the CD and proceed with your active imagination.

When you feel you've finished, just open your eyes and come back fully refreshed and relaxed.

> **An Important Note:** Should you encounter an experience that feels uncomfortable, before coming back, go to your "safe place" and stay there until you feel better. The "safe place" is an area in your imagination where you feel comfortable, protected, and safe. It is a part of your imagination or perhaps a memory of a place where you felt peaceful and out of harm's way. When you remember or revisit this safe place, focus on how you feel and what's going on around

you. Remember where you are and even if there is anyone there with you. In order to reexperience this safe place all you have to do is close your eyes, focus on your breathing, and go back to your protected space.

Exercise Three: Journal All of Your Reflections and Insights

In as much detail as possible, list all of the characteristics and positive themes that have occurred to you in the Active Imagination exercise. Journal any insights you have regarding their formation and function in these positive themes of your life. At this point you can refer to the list of positive complexes in Chapter Seven to further clarify your reflections. If you wish, make any drawings that represent what you've discovered so far in this process.

Exercise Four: The Personal 360 Analysis (Optional but Helpful)

This exercise draws on a technique used in management consulting to assess strengths and weaknesses of managers in organizations. It involves anonymously questioning subordinates, coworkers, and superiors regarding the management style of the subject. For our purposes, you can use this technique to get feedback from others close to you—family, friends, relatives, coworkers—regarding their opinion of your positive characteristics, themes, and complexes.

If you choose to use this exercise, send out an email or letter to a select group of people whom you feel know you and would be honest in responding to the following request:

Dear _____,
I am doing a serious introspective exercise regarding positive aspects of my personality. I would like your honest opinion.

What do you feel are my positive characteristics? Consider skills, talents, behaviors, attributes, strong points, values, philosophies, and ways of being. Be as detailed or as succinct as you like, but please be honest. Feel free to return your response without identifying yourself if you like.

Sincerely,

_____

Be sure to read any responses only *after* you've completed Exercises One and Two. You can then use the feedback from this 360 analysis to update and modify your own personal reflections from Exercises One and Two.

Should you see a characteristic that you disagree with or haven't considered, take note. Is this a characteristic that you're blind to or in denial about? Reflect on any new insights and make any adjustments to your time line with journal entries.

Exercise Five: Define Your Positive Themes and Complexes

In this exercise you'll further clarify and fine tune the list of positive complexes you've identified in the first three or four exercises.

- Group these positive characteristics into categories and similar themes.
- At this point, think about how these themes may be grouped into more specific categories.
- As you reflect on each characteristic, consider how it may be a part of the same theme.
  - o For example, the helper, caregiver, teacher, and generous character may all be different aspects of the theme of service to others.
  - o Define or label the theme or complex that reflects all of these subcharacteristics. Come up with the title or theme that feels best to you.
  - o Also, think about how a characteristic might be reduced to a more specific core characteristic or theme.
  - o Consider these questions: Is there a core theme of the characteristic of intelligence that might be more descriptive? Is the theme of high curiosity, good memory, or good integrator of information a better way to describe this positive complex?

Make a final definitive list of your positive complexes. Write in your journal any additional reflections or insights. Consider that some or all of these positive complexes may change or be further refined as you continue on with this journey of self-discovery.

Exercise Six: Zeroing In on Your Soul Purpose

As indicated in the intuitive readings of Edgar Cayce, soul purpose provides meaning, direction, and an overriding theme in one's current life. In the words of Dr. Mark Thurston, a contemporary Cayce scholar, "Your soul's purpose is a uniquely creative and dynamic approach to living. It involves special ways of reaching out to serve others and of reaching inward to nurture yourself."[9]

Our unique approach to living has everything to do with those positive aspects of ourselves—our positive complexes—that make up who we are. It is in soul purpose that some or all of these positive themes converge into a unifying theme that provides meaning and direction in life. Soul purpose may involve a vocation or avocation (something we do) or a way of being in the world (something we are). In any case, it is safe to say that there is a karmic or past-life history to our positive themes and soul purpose. In the next section, you'll explore the past-life background that informs and energizes your soul purpose in this life. You will gain further insights and clarity about how your unique positive complexes contribute to your personal life mission. For now, in this exercise, you'll focus on what you know about your unique approach to living in this life and how that involves the positive complexes you've identified.

Active Imagination Exercise to Explore Your Soul Purpose

Start by doing the same Active Imagination exercise described in Exercise Two. This time start with the intention of considering all of

---

[9]Mark Thurston, *Discovering Your Soul's Purpose* (Virginia Beach, VA: A.R.E. Press, 1984), back cover.

these positive themes and how they may serve as aspects of your soul purpose.

Once you're relaxed and before you proceed with the Active Imagination exercise, read through and reflect on the following suggestions:

- Consider how important these prominent complexes or themes have been in your life:
    - o Look at your relationships in all circumstances.
    - o Look at your schooling, training, and educational history.
    - o Look at your past and present work experience.
    - o Look at the hobbies and interests you have pursued.
    - o Look at your accomplishments and achievements.
    - o Look at your positive attitudes, values, philosophies, and ways of being.

- How has each of these complexes driven your life to date or provided satisfaction and meaning in your life or even given you a sense of purpose and joy?
- How does each of these complexes play out in your life today; how important are they; how purposefully do you exercise them day-to-day?
- Which would you like to develop, work with, or focus on more than ever?
- Consider how some or all of these positive complexes come together under a single central idea or unifying theme that seems to drive your life.
- Remember how you felt and what you were thinking when you were involved in doing something related to this unifying theme.
- Consider how this experience had in some way to do with service to others.
- Consider how, at times, some or all of these positive complexes have caused you difficulties, pain, suffering, discomfort, or frustration.

Proceed with the Active Imagination Exercise
- o Set the intention of exploring your sense of soul purpose.
- o Just as you did in the Active Imagination Exercise Two, start by playing the progressive relaxation exercise—Track One on the

enclosed CD. Again, you may choose to memorize the script and guide yourself into that relaxed state. Or, you may use the tape you've prepared for yourself.

○ Suspend all judgment and analysis.

○ Start your journey and be sure to engage in a dialogue when the opportunity presents itself.

○ When you're finished, journal your experience.

Exercise Seven: Journal Your Reflections and Write a Definitive Statement of Your Soul Purpose

Finish this part of your journey of self-exploration by writing a definitive statement that best describes your unifying theme—your soul purpose. We will refer to this as a mission statement in a later chapter. You can refer to the following examples of soul purpose statements for some ideas.

Examples of Soul Purpose Themes

Helping to motivate the undeveloped to mature

Celebrating the workings of God through nature

The appreciation and cultivation of nature

Synthesizing and blending

The innovator—getting new things started

Being a builder or a finisher who sees things through to completion

Sensitivity and support for the less fortunate ones in life

Bringing hope to others

Providing enabling guidance to those on a spiritual path

Nurturing my own spiritual development through an active spiritual practice and by helping others

Supporting, guiding, and nurturing the spiritual development of children

Demonstrating the workings of spirit through my work

Inspiring the spiritual development of others through the arts

Write out your statement in your journal and make any drawings that represent what you've discovered.

A Final Note

Remember that as you proceed with subsequent chapters, what you have discovered in this chapter is only a beginning. As you continue on this journey, expect that you will further define and clarify what you've learned. This is an ongoing process. It will continue to unfold, especially as you start to awaken the past–life karmic roots of these themes and aspects of your life.

Chapter **10**

Defining the
Negative
Themes

A t this point you should have a fairly good idea of those positive themes or complexes in your biographical life—those constellations that energize who you are and how you are in the world. It's time now to take stock of those disruptive complexes that can get in the way of the full expression of who you are. These are the complexes that interfere with fully exercising your positive aspects, especially in your pursuit of soul purpose.

Again, these are the themes and reactive behaviors that have at their core a feeling of inadequacy regarding not only specific abilities or characteristics but also values and ways of being. The examples we've talked about show how these complexes have formed as a result of challenging, threatening, traumatic, or simply diminishing experiences in our biographical life.

It's important to remember that a single experience in this life, or a past life, is enough to initiate or activate a negative karmic complex. In addition to this, we may experience only the symptoms or reactions to lesion incidents from a past life without any history of an associated traumatic experience in this life.

So, let's go on with this final step of self-reflection as preparation for the Integrate Imagery exercises in the next section. As you proceed with the following reflection and Active Imagination exercises, you can expect not only to clarify your understanding of these karmic patterns but also to gain an even deeper insight as to how the negative complexes function in your life.

Exercise One: Reflecting On the Negative Karmic Themes

Once again, go back to your autobiographical time line; this time, focus on the negative disruptive experiences in your biographical life.

Prepare for the exercise:
- Find a quiet and comfortable place where you can relax and reflect on your life—a place where you will not be disturbed.
- Have at hand your autobiographical time line and journal plus any drawing materials.
- Relax and take several deep breaths to let go of any tension or holding.

Start this reflective exercise by focusing on the following suggestions and questions:
- Review your autobiographical time line and all the journal entries you've made so far.
- Notate and reflect on any emotionally or physically traumatic experiences in your history.
- Think back to your childhood and your relationship with your parents.
  o Was one more supportive than the other?
  o Was one more conflictive than the other?
  o How did they relate to each other and how did they treat each other?

- How was your relationship with any siblings and extended family members?
  - What were those relationships like?
  - Did you ever feel challenged or non-supported?
- Think back to your experiences with friends, teachers, co-workers, etc.
  - What were the difficult experiences in those relationships?
- Reflect back through your history with significant others.
  - What were the difficult or challenging experiences in those relationships?
  - Are there patterns of behavior, circumstances, or experiences that are similar?
- Notice your routine reactions in certain situations.
  - When do you tend to get most aggressive, hostile, or combative?
  - When do you tend to get depressed, avoidant, or likely to withdraw?
  - When do you get fearful or anxious?
  - When do you feel most threatened, worried, or protective?
- Think about what might be considered your failures—in relationships, at school, at work, or in other parts of your life.
  - What were the circumstances?
- When do you feel inadequate or bad about yourself?
- What skills, characteristics, values, or ways of being do you feel inadequate about?
- What are you most fearful of?
- What are the circumstances today and in your past when you've felt sad, angry, guilty, ashamed, disgusted, or jealous?
- When do you get most defensive or protective?
- Have you heard others complaining about consistent traits, behaviors, or characteristics?
- What are the prominent and persistent scripts or thoughts that are troublesome, dysfunctional, or negative?
- Identify any prominent themes in your life. How were formed out of your life experience?

As you finish this reflective exercise, come up with a tentative list of your negative complexes with the associated feelings, scripts, sensations, and any reactive behaviors that come to you.

Exercise Two: Active Imagination on Your Negative Complexes

Just as you did in the Active Imagination exercise in the last chapter, start this process by setting an intention. Your intention in this exercise can be to explore specific feelings, scripts, thoughts, sensations, reactive behaviors, or themes that relate to traumatic, challenging, or difficult experiences in your biographical life. Or it can be to trust your unconscious mind to bring up an insight or experience regarding your negative complexes that is the most important for you to awaken.

Whatever you decide, again remember to suspend all judgment and analysis during the exercise and let the feelings, images, scripts, and physical sensations surface as you proceed. When you can, engage whatever surfaces by entering into a dialogue. You can actually ask questions of any characters, experiences, or situations that appear in order to gain further insight or understanding about these experiences. When you do, just wait for an answer.

Prepare for the exercise:
- Find a quiet and comfortable place where you can relax and reflect on your life—a place where you will not be disturbed.
- Have with you your autobiographical time line, journal, and any drawing materials.
- You can remember everything that occurs to you during this exploration.
- Close your eyes and take several deep relaxing breaths.
- When you're ready, start Track One on the enclosed CD with the progressive relaxation exercise—the same exercise you used in exploring your positive complexes and soul purpose. Again, you may choose to memorize the progressive relaxation script or prepare your own tape.
  - Allow yourself to move into a relaxing feeling of peace and calm—the same feeling you experienced in the prior Active Imagination exercises.

When you're ready, just go on to encounter any memory or experience that comes up. It's then that you may engage that memory, image, feeling, or thought with any questions. Just wait for a response.

- When you feel you've finished, come back to your safe place until you feel comfortable.
- Just open your eyes and feel refreshed and relaxed.

Exercise Three: Journal All Your Reflections and Insights

In as much detail as possible, list all of the characteristics, feelings, thoughts, sensations, and negative themes that have occurred to you in the Active Imagination exercise. Journal any insights that you have regarding these negative themes or complexes as well as their formation and function in your life. At this point it might be helpful to refer to the list of negative complexes in Chapter Six to further clarify your reflections. Make any drawings that represent what you've discovered so far in this process, if you wish. Don't forget to make notations on your autobiographical time line.

Exercise Four: How Your Negative Complexes Surface and Interact

In this reflective exercise you'll take an even closer look at all of the positive and negative complexes you've defined so far. You should get some insights as to how your own positive complexes can sometimes join up with each other as demonstrated in the examples in Chapter Eight. You'll look at how the negative can do the same and especially how the negative can make use of the positive as defensive or protective devices. Through this reflective process you may find yourself adding more to your list or even eliminating some complexes from your list as you continue to refine and deepen your understanding of your biographical current life.

Prepare for the exercise:
- Find a quiet and comfortable place where you can relax and reflect

on your life—a place where you will not be disturbed.
- Have at hand your autobiographical time line and journal plus any drawing materials. Be sure to have your entries and notes on positive complexes from the previous chapter.
- Relax and take several deep breaths to let go of any tension or holding.

Start this reflective exercise by focusing on the following suggestions or questions:
- Review your autobiographical time line and all the journal entries you've made so far.
- Go back to your list of positive complexes and the notes you made and once again reflect on how different positive skills, characteristics, and ways of being may come together or join forces under certain situations.
- Does the expression of any of these positive complexes sometimes seem to get you in trouble?
  - Do they create problems in your relationships?
  - Do they create problems at work or in other parts of your life?
- Do any positive complexes get exaggerated or overused at times?
  - Do any complexes seem to put you at a disadvantage when dealing with others or pursuing work or leisure time activities?
  - Do any complexes set you up to allow others to take advantage of you?
- Can you see how you've used some or all of these positive aspects to compensate or protect yourself from the feelings of inadequacy and sensitivities that come with your negative complexes?
- Can you see how two of your negative complexes can join forces at times? For example, an authority complex may join with an abandonment complex.

When you finish reflecting on these questions, once again summarize and journal your insights in preparation for the next exercise.

Exercise Five: Active Imagination to Explore How These Complexes Affect Each Other

In this exercise you'll set your intention to explore all of the interactive dynamics of those complexes that you are aware of as well as those that you have yet to define. Again, suspend all judgment and analysis during the exercise and let the feelings, images, scripts, physical sensations, and experiences surface as you proceed. When you can, engage whatever surfaces by entering into a dialogue. You can actually ask questions of any characters or situations that appear. When you do, just wait for an answer.

Prepare for the exercise:
- Find a quiet and comfortable place where you can relax and reflect on your life—a place where you will not be disturbed.
- Have with you your autobiographical time line, journal, and any drawing materials.
- You can remember everything that occurs to you during this exploration.
- Close your eyes and take several deep, relaxing breaths.

Use the same progressive relaxation exercise—on Track One on the enclosed CD—you used in the preceding Active Imagination exercises. Allow yourself to move into a relaxing feeling of peace and calm. Proceed with your active imagination, this time with the intention of gaining insight as to how the positive and negative complexes interact with, interfere with, or enliven each other. Reflect on your insights from the last exercise before you start your progressive relaxation exercise. Journal your experiences.

Exercise Six: Reflect On All of Your Positive and Negative Complexes as They Relate to Your Sense of Soul Purpose

In this final reflective exercise regarding your biographical current life experience, you'll be refining further your insights regarding both the positive and negative complexes. Most important, you'll look at how all of these aspects of yourself affect how you have experienced and pursue your unique sense of soul purpose.

From the preceding Active Imagination exercise and all that you've learned in this chapter, make a final definitive list of your negative complexes. Consider the following questions:

- What are the primary and secondary negative themes that play out in your life—ones that you've identified as complexes?
- What are the prominent feelings and scripts associated with these themes?
- Are there any associated physical sensations that come with each complex?
- How do they cause you to react when triggered?
- What is the biographical current life history of their formation and function?
- Now make a final definitive list of all of the negative complexes you've identified. Journal your insights and make any drawing you wish.

From what you have defined as your soul purpose so far, reflect on the following questions:

- How do your positive complexes contribute or influence your sense of soul purpose?
- How have or how could your negative complexes interfere with your pursuit of soul purpose?

Journal your insights in as much detail as possible.

Section Four:
Awakening Past Lives

You've spent the last two chapters in Section Three reflecting on the autobiographical time line of your current life. Now we're ready to awaken and explore the deeper karmic roots of those patterns, themes, or complexes that you have chosen—on a soul level—to bring into this life. Through the Integrated Imagery exercises, you'll have the opportunity to validate and process those past-life experiences that are here to be enlivened and those that are here to be resolved in the service of soul purpose. As important, you can expect to gain even deeper insight as to your unique sense of purpose in this life as you access the before-life state.

The four Integrated Imagery exercises that follow in the next two chapters will enable you to awaken the memories throughout your energetic chain of experience in this process of self-exploration. Now you'll use Tracks Two through Five on the prerecorded CD that will first guide you into a state of deep relaxation and then take you to a safe place and over a bridge to those past-life, between-life, before-life, and perinatal experiences that are the antecedents of the karmic patterns and complexes in this life.

Chapter **11**

Awakening the Positive Themes of Past Lives

We've spent a good amount of time focusing on your biographical current life, reflecting and defining the many positive and negative karmic patterns that constitute the personality that is "you." Part of this excursion of self-discovery has also focused on clarifying or perhaps awakening for the first time that unique personal dimension which is soul purpose.

From here on we'll be concentrating on those prior-life experiences that most likely are antecedents to these characteristics or karmic patterns that you bring to this life. The purpose of the self-guided Integrated Imagery exercises that follow:

- To gain deeper insight as to the formation and most important, the function of these enlivening and disruptive karmic patterns that we bring into this life.
- In the process to enliven or accentuate the positive patterns.
- To start the process of de-energizing the negative patterns.

- To facilitate the learning experience in this immediate life experience.
- And finally to clear the path for your personal pursuit of soul purpose.

A Few Reminders

In the first section we talked about the energetic chain of experience, which is made up of not only past-life and biographical-life, but also between-life, before-life, and perinatal (or in utero) experiences. As we've discussed at length, the fact remains that our karmic patterns or complexes which form in a given past life or lives will consistently be reflected in some way in our between/before-life states as well as in the perinatal or in utero aspect of this life. Each time the karmic pattern surfaces in our day-to-day life, it tends to add to or reinforce the positive or negative aspects of the complex in the karmic pattern and accumulate energy as it lives on and grows.

For example, the Bedouin elder dies with a feeling of abandonment that carries into his between-life existence. He may have had similar experiences in other lives. In the between-life state there is the opportunity to reflect on one or more of these past-life experiences to gain further insight as to which complexes are carried forward. On a soul level, it is in the before-life state that Ben decides to carry in this abandonment theme to deal with and resolve in this life. That abandonment theme then was carried through each level of his energetic chain.

Let's not forget that the same holds true for positive complexes. We are likely to see the thread of those positive characteristics in each level of the energetic chain. It is by awakening the memories in these different dimensions of experience that we gain deeper understanding as to the formation and function of our complexes—how they affect our current lives and how we may grow through this understanding.

The approach then in doing the following self-directed Integrated Imagery exercises is to accentuate the positive and de-energize the negative as we clarify and empower our personal pursuit of soul purpose. Regarding the accentuation of the positive complexes, this amounts to uncovering the many dimensions of our positive skills, abilities, values, and ways of being and essentially accepting the fact that these are parts of who we have been and who we are in the world. It is about accepting ownership and gaining confidence that we may continue to grow those positive parts of our personality.

With the negative karmic complexes it's a slightly different story. In these cases it's more a matter of finishing the unfinished business of the past, which involves saying and doing the unsaid and undone. It also involves releasing the physical imprints that the body holds. And it requires changing the negative thoughts and scripts that result from those wounding experiences of the past. So let us begin this awakening process and your excursion through the energetic chain of experience.

One Important Note before You Begin

It's important for you at this point to make a serious commitment to your personal process of self-discovery. Engage each exercise in this chapter and the next to its fullest. Even if you feel at first that this process is not working exactly the way you thought, be persistent. Trust in this awakening process. These are time-proven exercises that can provide insight, healing, and a very positive force in your life. The techniques that you'll learn in the following pages can be used for the rest of your life as you continue to grow and evolve. Have faith and be persistent. You are bound to be surprised.

In addition, these self-guided regression exercises are not meant to take the place of individual regression work with a qualified, trained regression therapist. There may be issues that you might want to consider dealing with in one-on-one work with a qualified therapist. Should you experience any lasting negative effects from any regression experience or if you feel stuck regarding a specific incident or insight, seek out professional help.

An Overview of the Exercises Ahead

The next four exercises, in this chapter and the next, are designed to help you explore your own energetic chain of experience with the idea of awakening those memories for healing and growth—for spiritual development.

Integrated Imagery Exercise One, (Track Two on the CD), guides you back to the past lives underlying your positive complexes. What is the origin of those positive themes? How did they form and function in the past? How are they a part of your life today? It is by revisiting the enlivening experiences in your past that you may gain deeper insight as to the positive aspects of who you are in this life. By doing so, you can start to refocus your current life on those abilities and ways of being that will lead to a more fulfilling life.

In the Integrated Imagery Exercise Two (Track Three on the CD) in the next chapter, you'll concentrate on the past-life roots of the negative dysfunctional complexes that plague your life. What is their past-life history? What deeper insights can you gain regarding their disruptive effects? How have they interfered with your well-being and pursuit of your passion in this life? How can you put them to rest?

In each of these Integrated Imagery experiences you'll be guided through the progressive relaxation exercise to enter the past-life at some point and to process through the significant experiences until you move through the death experience and into the between-life state. At that point you'll have the opportunity to connect the experiences in that past life with your biographical life. How do these past-life experiences continue to play out in both positive and negative ways? It is during this between-life state that you can expect to gain even deeper insight into the workings of these complexes and themes. It is by revisiting or re-experiencing these traumatic episodes in the past that you can bring them into consciousness. And it is by re-visioning the outcome of those experiences in a positive way and finishing the unfinished business that you may release the hold they have on this life.

In the Integrated Imagery Exercise Three (Track Four on the CD) in the next chapter, you'll be exploring the implications of soul purpose. The objective of this aspect of awakening is to go back to a past life or past lives that are roots of your unique mission. Most important in this exercise is the regression back to the before-life state—to the time of decision-making and preparation for the entrance into the this life. This may be the time for engaging spirit guides; for observing parents, siblings, or family members, and even for deciding on the astrological configuration you are to be born into. In any case, it is the time that we decide—as Edgar Cayce indicated—on the positive and negative karmic patterns that we bring into this life.

All three of these regression exercises can and should be repeated any number of times, at will, as you progress through your process of awakening. Each time you can expect to gain deeper insight as you resolve the unfinished business of the past and enliven those positive themes.

The Integrated Imagery Exercise Four (Track Five on the CD) has you focus on the perinatal aspect of the energetic chain. This will take you back into early childhood and then into the time between conception and your actual birth. This is where we see the first imprints of those past–life patterns and where you'll start to gain further insight into the function of these aspects of "self."

The Four Steps in Each Integrated Imagery Exercise

The *first step*, as you start the following Integrated Imagery exercises, is to set a clear intention, just as you did in the preceding Active Imagination exercises. That intention can be as indirect as accessing a past–life or prior–life experience that will give you some insight as to the issues to explore. In this case, it's a matter of trusting your unconscious mind to take you to a memory that will be helpful for you to awaken.

As you progress, it will be advisable and more helpful to set your intention to explore more specific issues. This could involve going back through a specific feeling or emotion that is persistent in your current life. A feeling of anger or fear or a feeling of guilt or jealousy could be important starting points to your regression process. On the other side a feeling of joy, passion, excitement, or any other positive emotion could serve as a bridge into a past life that would be an antecedent to something going on in your life today. You might intend to explore a specific script or thought that has been a source of discomfort or joy. "I'm not good enough"; "I'll always be alone," or "I love to do _____" are just a few examples. You could focus on a particular physical sensation like a chronically sore back or a physical disability that you think might have some connection with a positive or negative karmic pattern. Finally, you can decide to explore an image, for example, out of a dream, other regression experiences, or out of a memory in your past. As you proceed with your regression exercises, it's important, regardless of the intention you set, just to allow the regression experiences to unfold without judgment or analysis. It's equally important to be patient and persistent as you progress through each regression experience.

After setting the intention, the *second step* is to find a quiet, comfortable place where you can relax without being disturbed. Once again, the Tracks Two through Five on the enclosed CD are recordings of my voice to guide you through each of the four regression experiences that follow. For each of these regression sessions it will be helpful to read through the transcripts in Appendix B before you start the exercise—just so you are familiar with the process. Again, you have the option of preparing your own tapes using the following scripts, just as in the preceding Active Imagination exercises.

When you are ready, start playing the CD or the tape. Each session will begin by guiding you through a progressive relaxation exercise to help you move into a deeper state of relaxation and trance. The script then takes you to your safe place and then to the bridge that will indicate the suggestion to go back into a past-life or before-life state to explore your intention.

Once you're in the past-life or before-life experience, the next step involves the actual process you'll go through as you explore the experience. Each of the following exercises guides you through specific experiences in the past to enable you to gain insight, enliven the positive, and de-energize the negative themes and complexes.

In the case of a past-life memory, once you're in the life, you'll start by getting clear about who you are and what's going on around you. You'll be encouraged to move into the personality or character and to become that person. Then move through as many significant events in that life as you can so that you start to understand the relevance of that life and its impact on this life. Finally, you'll move through the death experience until you're out of body and in the between-life state. Remember that what we experience in the process of dying can have the most significant impact on the karmic imprints we take out of that life. The between-life experience after the death, again, is where we may gain even deeper insight as to the influence of that life. This is also where we can most effectively integrate these memories.

An Important Suggestion: When playing the enclosed CD or your pre–recorded tape, it's advisable to keep your finger on the pause button during the regression. This will give you the opportunity to stop the recording to allow you the time you need to experience whatever comes up. When you're ready to move on with other experiences, just push the play button to continue. You can do this without interrupting the altered state you have achieved. Now, carry on with your journey of awakening.

Integrated Imagery Exercise One (Track Two): Awakening the Roots of Your Positive Themes

The transcript in the Appendix B is what I used on the enclosed CD. Again, read through the script so that you're familiar with the process you'll be experiencing.

If you're preparing a tape in your own voice or someone else's, use this same transcript to guide you through this self-regression process. When preparing the tape, remember to speak slowly—in a monotone voice—and to pay attention to the indications of a pause.

When you're ready, proceed with the following steps as you start to explore the roots of your positive complexes.

- In a quite reflective state *set your intention*. For example, to:
  - ○ Explore any past life that will give you insight into your positive complexes.
  - ○ Explore specific feelings, images, scripts, sensations, behaviors, or activities that relate to those positive themes.
  - ○ Deepen your insight into those talents, skills, characteristics, values, or ways of being.

When you finish your regression, journal your experience in as much detail as possible. Make any drawings that would represent your experience.

Remember that you can go back to this Integrated Imagery exercise at any time to continue to explore other positive complexes or to deepen your insight regarding the positive themes you've already explored. Take as much time as you need before going on.

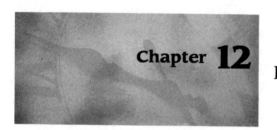

Chapter **12**

Exploring the Rest of the Energetic Chain of Experience

N ow that you've spent some time delving into the roots of those positive aspects of who you are, it's time to awaken the past–life antecedents of those negative themes and to explore the rest of the energetic chain. These are the themes that disrupt your relationships and contribute to the dysfunction in your life. They can be at the root of not only behavioral, psychological, and emotional problems in your life but also of the physical symptoms that you may have been dealing with. They are the patterns that can turn the positive complexes into troublesome behaviors. And they are the aspects of you that invariably interfere with the mission of actualizing your soul purpose. Let's continue this journey of awakening by focusing on the deeper past–life roots of these negative themes.

Integrated Imagery Exercise Two (Track Three): Exploring the Negative Complexes

To start the exercise, review the transcript for Track Three in Appendix B. As you can see from the transcript, the difference in this exercise is that the processing and closure stages will involve awakening these past-life and between-life experiences to de-energize them as well as to understand their implications in this life. This may call for taking yourself back into the death experience or parts of that life several times to redo your behavior and your reactions and to fully release those experiences—all towards resolution.

If you are held hostage, for example, you can go back into that experience and imagine yourself getting away. If you were harmed or helpless in any way, you can imagine yourself fighting back and this time doing what wasn't possible in that past life.

On the other hand, if you were a perpetrator—harming others or causing emotional or psychological pain—the resolution may come from stopping yourself and asking for forgiveness. In the final analysis, the resolution comes from finishing the unfinished business, correcting behaviors, making amends, and writing the wrongs of the past.

Remember that the negative complex may be out of a retributive karmic reaction where you were the perpetrator in the past and now end up being the victim. Or it may be a continuitive reaction where you were and continue to be the victim. Either way, closure during this self-directed regression session will come out of your efforts to balance that negative experience with a compensating positive reaction. This is all in the process of learning and soul growth.

Proceed with the Integrated Imagery Exercise on Track Three

- Find a quiet and comfortable place where you won't be disturbed.
- Take some time to establish your intention for this Integrated Imagery exercise. Again, this can be to explore a particular feeling, script, image, physical sensation, or negative theme in your life—especially an issue that has come out of the autobiographical time line or Ac-

tive Imagination exercises. The intention could also be to simply open to your unconscious mind and explore any prior experience that will provide insight and healing.

- When you're ready, start the CD or tape and remember to have an easy way to stop and start the recorded guiding script if you need more time to process and experience.

- When you finish your regression, journal your experience in as much detail as possible. Make any drawings that would represent your experience.

Remember that you can go back to this Integrated Imagery exercise at any time to continue to explore other complexes or to deepen your insight regarding the negative themes and complexes you've already explored. Take as much time as you need to analyze these negative karmic themes before you go on to the next exercise.

Integrated Imagery Exercise Three (Track Four): Awakening Your Soul Purpose Memories

Now it's time to go back to the spirit state of consciousness, just before this life, to awaken the insights you may get regarding your unique sense of mission in this life—your soul purpose. Before you proceed with this regression exercise, review all of your reflections from the exercises in the preceding chapters. What have you discovered or realized so far?

This Integrated Imagery exercise will take you back to the before–life state. As the laws of karma and the Cayce readings indicate, the karmic patterns (complexes) and the unique purpose that you carry into this life have been decided on by you and you alone. You may get help and direction from spirit guides, but the final decisions as to the lessons and mission in this life have been up to you. These decisions were made just prior to entering this life.

To prepare for the exercise, read again the transcript for Track Four in Appendix B to make sure you are familiar with how you will be guided.

Proceed with the Integrated Imagery Exercise to Explore Your Soul Purpose

- When you're ready to start the CD or tape, find a quiet and comfortable place where you won't be disturbed.
- Take some time to establish your intention for this Integrated Imagery exercise. This time the intention is to explore and gain deeper insight as to your unique sense of soul purpose in this life.
- When you're ready, start the CD and remember to have an easy way to stop and start the recorded guiding script if you need more time to process and experience.
- When you finish your regression, journal your experience in as much detail as possible. Make any drawings that would represent your experience.
- This is a time when you can further clarify the mission statement you prepared in earlier exercises. After completing this Integrated Imagery exercise, you should gain some insight and clarity. Again, remember this is an exercise you can revisit many times. Each time you can expect to learn more about the questions you've asked. Be patient—be persistent.

Integrated Imagery Exercise Four (Track Five): Awakening Perinatal Memories

Remember that your energetic chain of experience includes the time that you spent in utero—between conception and birth. Even though we are not fully formed physical beings, this is a time when we can experience what is going on in the outside world. These are experiences that can still have an impact on our current lives in positive and negative ways. It also a time when we have a direct link into what our mother and father are thinking and feeling—how they are experiencing their own lives and anticipating our birth. It is a time when their life experiences may actually be perceived as our own. What they're feeling, thinking, and sensing may be taken in as our own. And, it is a time when we can get a direct sense of the experiences of our siblings and other family members.

Most important, it is a time when our past-life karmic patterns and that sense of soul purpose are first imprinted on our emotional and physical bodies that are forming in utero. These can be the first inklings of the themes or complexes that will play out in this life. By awakening these perinatal memories, we can gain even deeper insight as to the themes we carry into this life as we move toward accentuating the positive and de-energizing the negative.

Proceed with the Integrated Imagery Exercise Four (Track Five on the CD) to Explore Your Perinatal Experience

- Find a quiet and comfortable place where you won't be disturbed.
- Take some time to establish your intention for this Integrated Imagery exercise. This time the intention is to explore your perinatal before birth or in utero experience and to gain deeper insight as to how that affects your life today.
- When you're ready, start Track Five on the CD—Integrated Imagery Session Four—or your own prepared tape and remember to have an easy way to stop and start the recorded guiding script if you need more time to process and experience.
- When you finish your regression, journal your experience in as much detail as possible. Make any drawings that would represent your experience.
- Again, remember that this is an exercise you can revisit many times. Each time you can expect to learn more about the questions you've asked. Be patient—be persistent.

One Final Thought

These four Integrated Imagery exercises were designed to enable you to explore your entire energetic chain of experience and to awaken those memories that have formed the karmic patterns and complexes that you have carried into this life. Now take some reflective time to clarify even further who you are and who you have been. As you engage this reflective process, you can expect to continue to accentuate the positive and de-energize the negative. This is the time to make full use of the free will with which we are all blessed. What changes can you make regarding how you engage in life: the way you react, the way you feel, what you think? In light of the memories you have awakened, what can you do to improve and enhance your experience in this life? How can you fully accept and pursue your life purpose and make the most of the gift that is the rest of this life?

One Final Exercise in Your Process of Awakening

Now that you have the tools to continue to explore the many aspects of who you have been and who you are in this life, there is one final reflective exercise that can be helpful.

- When you're ready, find a quiet and peaceful place to relax and reflect on your life to date and what you've learned.
- Look over your autobiographical time line—this time taking a much broader perspective. Consider your entire life as a continuous process with all of these incidents, experiences, and phases as interconnected—the easy and difficult, the positive and negative, the accomplishments and failures.
- Reflect back over the positive events in your life. How have they contributed to where you are today? Consider your childhood years, your relationships, your accomplishments, your adult experiences, etc.
- Now, look at those difficult experiences and times. Think about how even those times in your life have contributed to the positive aspects of who you are today and how you live your life. You may have to work at this a bit. How have these difficult passages in your life brought you to your present state of awakening? The truth is that no matter how easy or difficult the process has been, your entire life process is moving in a positive direction toward growth, learning, and fulfillment.
- Reflect on how all of these experiences in your life are interconnected.
- Now is the time to be grateful not only for the good times but also for the challenging experiences. You now have the tools to continue this journey of self-discovery.

Enjoy the trip and be well!

An Afterthought

Chapter 13

As you continue to work with the exercises in this book, there are several other sources of information that you might want to consider.

Psychic Readings Regarding Your Past Lives

The information from psychic, intuitive, or channeled readings can lend an even deeper insight as to the influence of past lives on your biographical life. The Edgar Cayce life readings are a good example of how helpful such a reading might be in your own process of self-discovery. In more than fourteen thousand readings subjects gained insight and healing regarding not only physical disorders but also the psycho-emotional and spiritual aspects of their lives. Such a reading can be used as a starting point in your awakening process. The advantage you have is that now you have the tools to carry on the process through your own self-guided regression exercises.

A reading with a qualified intuitive or psychic can also be valuable in validating, redirecting, and advancing the process you've already started. What is important to emphasize is that you find a professional with proven experience and a psycho-spiritual orientation. For guidance in finding someone with those qualifications, I suggest that you contact the Association for Research and Enlightenment in Virginia Beach. Check the Web site at www.edgarcayce.org.

Astrological Readings

Another outside source of information and guidance can come from an astrological reading. Again, the experience, qualifications, and orientation of the astrological counselor are critical. One with not only a metaphysical/spiritual but also a psychological orientation can provide insight as to your positive and negative—the challenging and enlivening—themes, characteristics, tendencies, and ways of being that may enlighten and possibly initiate your discovery process.

In essence, the entire natal chart that we are born with, as well as the progressed chart that evolves during our lives, is reflecting a karmic imprint. It is through such a reading that the past-life roots and before-life decisions regarding that unique sense of soul purpose may also be uncovered. What is important to understand is that the interpretation of the influence of our astrological alignment at the time of birth and throughout our lives is a complicated affair. In order to gain the most from such a reading, the entire natal chart (and ultimately the progressed chart) with its many interactive aspects must be considered. Because of this complexity, the qualifications and approach of the astrological counselor is important.

One more point to consider is that it's important to remember the guidance from the Cayce readings. Astrology cannot be predictive concerning one's course or destiny in life. A reading cannot tell you how you will behave or react to the circumstances in life. Nor can it predict the final outcome. Cayce alluded to the idea that astrology is 20 per cent; free will is 80 per cent. The course your life will take is up to you. What makes the difference is how aware you are of the karmic themes that constitute your deep sense of "self." The exercises you've experienced throughout this book have been designed to provide you with the opportunity to raise your awareness. An astrological reading, then, could be considered another tool to help stimulate your awakening experience.

Finally, the objective of this book has been to enable you to uncover and start the process of resolving those dysfunctional themes (or complexes) and to accentuate those positive themes (or complexes) that contribute to your mission of soul development. This should be considered a beginning. Each of these exercises can and should be revisited as you continue your personal process of self-discovery. You can expect to gain deeper insight each time you revisit any of these exercises. This awakening process is ongoing. There is always the possibility of learning and growth. That's the good news. And there is no bad news. You now have proven tools to enhance your life.

I would be remiss if I did not suggest another way of continuing your awakening experience. That option includes finding a qualified past-life regression therapist. This can be helpful if you feel you've reached a stuck spot or a block regarding a specific issue. This can also be helpful in simply advancing the work you've already done. Although you can gain a great deal of insight by following the exercises in this book, there may be times when professional guidance can be important.

For now, good luck on your journey of awakening and self-discovery!

Diagrams

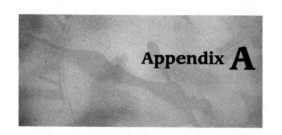

Appendix A

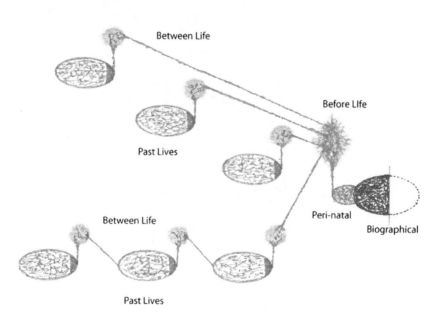

Diagram 1: The Energetic Chain of Experience

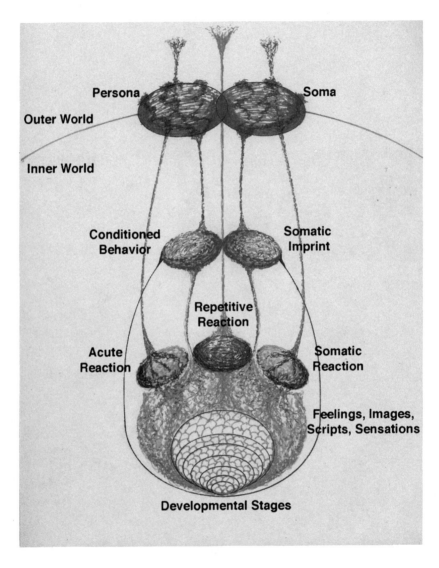

Diagram 2: The Complex Mechanism

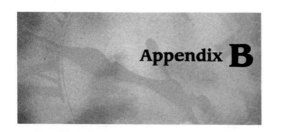

Transcripts of the Integrated Imagery Exercises on the CD

Track One: The Progressive Relaxation Exercise

And now we will proceed with this exercise of self-discovery through a progressive relaxation exercise that will allow you to release any tension and move into that deeper state of relaxation and trance.

So, when you're ready, just find a comfortable place to relax the body. And you can close your eyes now. And just start to scan the body. Be aware of any places of tension you're holding, and through the breath, just release that tension or holding.

> Now, bring your attention down to your feet and calves and thighs. Be aware of any tension or holding, and just let it go, through the breath.
>
> Now, focus on your lower back and spinal column and shoulders. Be aware of tension or holding, and just let it go, through the breath.

Now, focus on your abdomen and chest and throat. Be aware of any tension or holding, and just let it go, through the breath.

Focus on your neck and lower jaw and facial area. Be aware any tension or holding. And just let it go, through the breath.

Now, you can move into a deeper state of relaxation and trance, and you can continue to release any tension or holding.

In your mind's eye now, take yourself to a place either out of your imagination or a place where you've been. This is a place where you can feel safe, protected, where nothing can harm you or cause any discomfort. This is your safe place. So take some time to relax into that place before you go on.

Pause for at least 15 seconds.

Notice what's going on around you. Notice how you feel—relaxed and safe.

Notice what kind of day it is. And you can start to move around in this place, feeling comfortable and safe.

Just take all the time you need to relax and let go of any tension or holding. And when you're ready, you can go on to encounter any memory or experience that comes up.

And it's then that you can engage that memory, the images, the feelings, the thoughts, and any questions.

Pause

It's now that you can wait for a response.

Now you can proceed with your intention to explore and to gain insight about your themes and complexes.

Track Two: Awakening the Roots of Your Positive Themes

And now for this first integrated imagery session you can start by relaxing into a deeper state of the consciousness. We'll start by focusing on the breath.

Just be aware of the incoming breath and the outgoing breath, taking in that sense of relaxation and trance, and letting go of any tension or holding.

And now, scan the body and be aware of any places of tension; through the breath release that tension and start to relax.

And now focus on your feet, and calves, and thighs. Be aware of any tension and just let it go, through the breath.

Now, focus on your lower back and spinal column and shoulders. Be aware of any tension, and just let it go, through the breath.

Now, focus on your abdomen and chest and throat. Be aware of any tension, and just let it go, through the breath.

Now, focus on your neck and lower jaw and facial area. Be aware of any tension, and let it go, through the breath.

Now, be more and more relaxed as you move into that deeper state of awareness and trance.

You may be aware of that deeper state of relaxation coming over you as you notice your breathing getting easier and parts of your body relaxing more and more or your body sinking into the cushion.

Whatever you notice, just relax into that deeper state of awareness.

Pause for at least 15 seconds.

Now, in your mind's eye, go to a place either out of your imagi-nation or a place you've been.

This is a place where you can feel safe and protected, where nothing can harm you or cause any discomfort.

Just relax in that place for a time before you go on.

Pause for at least 15 seconds.

Be aware of what's going on around you, in this safe place.

What kind of day is it? **Pause.** *Is there anyone there?* **Pause.**

Most important, notice how relaxed you feel. **Pause.**

Now, as you look around, you'll see a path. Take whatever time you need to find that path. **Pause for 15 seconds.**

Start to see that path now . . . and when you do, start to move along the path, still feeling safe and protected. **Pause for 10 seconds.**

And as you look ahead, you'll start to see the bridge. That's the bridge that will take you back in time, to another place, to an-other life, one that will help you to understand some of the positive karma that you bring into this life, positive experiences out of your past lives. **Pause for 10 seconds.**

Now, as you approach the bridge and step onto the bridge, start to move slowly towards the other end. I'll count from one to twenty, as you move across the bridge, and at twenty, you can step off the bridge into a different time and place.

Starting to count now, stepping onto the bridge, one, two, three, four, five, six,

Moving over the bridge, seven, eight, nine, ten, eleven,

Halfway across the bridge, twelve, thirteen, fourteen, fifteen, sixteen, seventeen,

Approaching the end, eighteen, nineteen, twenty, stepping off the bridge onto the ground,

And now, start to be aware of where you are. Just look around. And take some time to realize where you are. **Pause for 10 seconds.**

You can start by looking down at your feet to see what you're wearing.

Are you wearing shoes or sandals? Are your feet bare?

And now, bring your awareness up your body and notice what you're wearing. **Pause.**

Are you a male or female?

Now notice what's going on around you as you look around.

Who's there with you?

And now, move on to the place where you live or the place where you're staying tonight and who is there. **Pause.**

Be aware of their relationships to you.

And notice how you're feeling. **Pause.**

Notice what you're thinking. **Pause.**

Notice what you sense in your body. **Pause.**

And be aware of any images that appear to you. **Pause.**

Now, at the count of three, move on to the next significant experience in that life—an experience that will give you insight into your intention. One, two, three.

What's happening now? What are you doing? **Pause.**

How are you interacting with other people?

Take some time to understand what's going on, how it relates to your positive themes.

Just be more and more aware of the positive experiences you're having. **Pause.**

And when you're ready, move on to the next significant experience. I'll count to three. One, two, three.

What's happening now? Where are you?

Again, notice how you are feeling, what you're thinking.

Notice what you sense in the body. **Pause.**

What's happening now? **Pause.**

Notice the positive aspects of this experience.

Now, you can start to gain some insight into how it relates to this life. But what's most important is that you fully experience what's going on. **Pause.**

And now, at the count of three, move ahead again, to the next significant experience in that life. One, two, three.

And now what's happening? Again, notice your feelings, the images.

Notice your thoughts, and notice what you hear from others.

Be aware of what you sense in the body. **Pause.**

And now you can move onto to as many significant, positive experiences as you can. **Pause.**

Now, when you're ready, move to the moments leading up to the death in that life.

Pause for 15 seconds.

What are you thinking and feeling now?

What do you sense in the body?

What's happening around you? **Pause.**

Who are the people with you? **Pause.**

What are they thinking and feeling?

What are they saying? **Pause.**

Now, as you slowly move through these last moments, you can start to feel yourself moving out of the body, above the body, higher and higher, until you can look down on the body you just left.

And as you do, continue to move higher and higher, until you can look down onto that entire life. **Pause.**

And now you can reflect as you move to that higher level of awareness.

You can reflect on that past life, and this life. Reflect on the connections between the two lives. **Pause.**

What is it that you carry from that life?

What are the feelings and images and thoughts and sensations that you carry with you? **Pause.**

Are there any people that are with you now from that life? **Pause.**

And most importantly, what are the themes that come out of that past-life experience? **Pause.**

This is a time when you can even gain deeper insight as to the connections, as to the positive themes, in this life, the positive skills and talents, the ways of being.

And you can expect some surprising insights. But, whatever comes to you in this between-life state, be aware of how you can enliven these positive themes in this life.

How you can draw on them, make use of them?

Just take some time to reflect and gain these insights. **Pause for 15 seconds.**

And now, when you're ready, you can start to slowly count back from ten to one.

Slowly come back into this body, into this time,

> *Come back to a state where you are alert and refreshed, bringing back these memories and insights with you.*
>
> *And just know that if there has been anything uncomfortable in that experience, you can leave it behind,*
>
> *With each count, come back.*
>
> *Starting to come back then . . . Ten, nine, eight, seven, six, five, four, three, two, one.*

Now, just take some time and reflect on this experience. You can journal what you remember, make any drawings you see fit. And if any additional insights come to you as you journal and reflect, be sure to make note of them.

Track Three: Exploring the Negative Complexes

Now that you've spent some time delving into the roots of those positive aspects of who you are, it's time to awaken the past–life experiences of negative themes and to explore the rest of the energetic chain. These are the themes that disrupt your relationships and contribute to the dysfunction in your life. Perhaps they are at the root of your behavioral, psychological, and emotional problems. They may also be the cause of the physical symptoms that you have been struggling with.

These are the complexes that can turn those positive complexes into troublesome behaviors, and they are the aspects of your personality that invariably interfere with the mission of actualizing your soul purpose.

Let's continue this journey of awakening by focusing on the deeper past–life routes of these negative themes. It's important to remember as you embark on this next stage of your journey that uncovering these negative themes and complexes must end by focusing on finishing the unfinished business of the past.

So, when you're ready, just find a relaxing place to recline, and start to focus on the breath, noticing the incoming breath and the outgoing breath, taking in that sense of relaxation and trance, and letting go of any tension or holding.

So, now scan the body and be aware of any places of tension.

Through the breath, release that tension and start to relax. **Pause.**

Again, focus on your feet and calves and thighs. Be aware of any tension or holding, and just let it go, through the breath.

Now, focus on your lower back and spinal column and shoulders. Be aware of any tension or holding, and just let it go, through the breath.

Now, focus on your abdomen and chest and throat. Be aware of any tension or holding, and just let it go, through the breath.

Now, focus on your neck and lower jaw and facial area. Be aware of any tension or holding, and just let it go, through the breath.

Now, you can be more and more relaxed as you move into that deeper state of awareness and trance.

You may be aware of that deeper state of relaxation coming over you as you notice your breathing getting easier or parts of the body relaxing more and more or the body sinking into the cushion.

Whatever you notice, just relax into that deeper state of awareness. **Pause for 10 seconds.**

Now, in your mind's eye, go to that safe place.

Again, a place out of your imagination or a place you've been.

This is a place where you can feel safe or protected, where nothing can harm you or cause you discomfort. **Pause.**

So, just relax into that place for a time before you go on. And be aware of what's going on around you, what kind of day it is. **Pause for 10 seconds.**

Is there anyone there? Notice how relaxed you feel. **Pause.**

Now, as you move around in the safe place, you'll see a path ahead of you. So take whatever time you need to find that path. **Pause.**

You can start to see that path now.

And when you do, start to move along that path, still feeling safe and protected.

And as you look ahead, you'll start to see the bridge. That's the bridge that will take you back in time, to another place, to another life.

One that will help you to understand some of the positive and, perhaps, troublesome karmic patterns that you bring into this life. **Pause.**

Now, as you approach the bridge, and step onto the bridge, you'll start to move slowly towards the other end.

I'll start to count from one to twenty as you move across the bridge. At one, stepping onto the bridge. At twenty, you'll step off the bridge into a different time and place.

One, onto the bridge, two, three, four, five, six; moving over the bridge, seven, eight, nine, ten, eleven,

Half way across the bridge, twelve, thirteen, fourteen, fifteen, sixteen, seventeen,

Approaching the end of the bridge, eighteen, nineteen, twenty; stepping off the bridge onto the ground.

Start to be aware of where you are; what's going on around you. **Pause for 10 seconds.**

Now, look down at your feet and see what you're wearing. Are you wearing shoes or sandals? Are your feet bare? **Pause.**

Now, bring your awareness up your body, and notice the clothes that you're wearing.

Are you a male or a female? **Pause.**

Turn your attention now to what's going on around you. Is there anyone there? **Pause.**

Can you hear voices?

How are you feeling?

What do you sense in the body? **Pause.**

Now, at the count of three, move on to the place where you live or where you'll be staying. One, two, three.

Who's there? **Pause.** *Notice how you're feeling now, what you're thinking, what you sense in the body,*

And, be aware of any images that appear to you. **Pause for 10 seconds.**

Be aware of what's going on. **Pause.**

And now, at the count of three, move onto the next significant experience in that life, an experience that will give you insight into your intention. One, two, three. What's happening now? What are you doing? **Pause for 10 seconds.**

Are you interacting with other people?

Take some time to understand what's going on. **Pause for 15 seconds.**

Are you feeling threatened, endangered?

How are you feeling about what's happening to you and what's going on around you? **Pause for 10 seconds.**

What are you thinking?

How are you feeling about what you're doing or about what someone else is doing? **Pause for 10 seconds.**

When you're ready, move on to the next significant experience. One, two, three.

What's happening now? Ask yourself the same questions as before, about what you are doing, how you are feeling, what you're thinking and sensing. **Pause for 10 seconds.**

What do you hear from others, and what do you observe of their behavior. **Pause for 10 seconds.**

Now you can decide to move on to as many significant experiences as you wish.

You can even pause to allow yourself the time to understand these experiences.

So, take whatever time you need. **Pause for 15 seconds or more. This is where you may stop the recording to process the experiences.**

Now, before moving on, you can move to a significant experience that would explain how this life affects your current life.

Just take some time now to understand and gain insight. **Pause for 10 seconds.**

And when you're ready, move to the moments leading up to the death in that life. **Pause.**

What's happening? What are you thinking and feeling now?

What sensations do you notice in your body?

What's happening around you? Who is with you? **Pause for 10 seconds.**

Now, whatever's happening as you move through the death experience, remember that your actual body is safe and protected.

Allow yourself now to move through the feelings and thoughts and images and experiences of dying in the past. **Pause.**

And, as you do, move to the moments of that last breath until you feel yourself moving out of the body, higher and higher, until you can look down on the body you just left. **Pause.**

Notice what's happening.

As you move out of the body into the between-life state, notice what you carry with you from that life—the feelings and thoughts, perhaps uncomfortable or threatening, the sensa-

tions in the physical body. **Pause for 10 seconds.**

Continue to move higher and higher until you can look down on that life and this life, until you can reflect on the connections between these two lives. **Pause.**

What is it that you carry from that life? **Pause.**

Are there any people that are in both lives? **Pause.**

Were you a victim of others or a victim of circumstances? **Pause.**

Were you the perpetrator, the victimizer? **Pause.**

And most important, what feelings do you carry with you? Anger, or fear, guilt, shame, disgust?

Are there other feelings? **Pause.**

What are the thoughts and words that you carry over from that life? **Pause.**

And, where do you hold this life, in your body now?

Take some time now to reflect, to gain further insights. **Pause for 10 seconds.**

And now, do what you must, before you come back, to right the wrongs, to finish the unfinished, to say what was unsaid, do what was undone. **Pause.**

Complete this story, this past life, in a positive way. **Pause.**

Now, when you can forgive your abusers, you can let go of those circumstances.

You can release this story of the past. **Pause.**

Now is when you can ask forgiveness of those who you've hurt or harmed.

You might see them before you; ask for their forgiveness. And accept that forgiveness.

Take whatever time you need to release this life, to finish what was unfinished. **Pause for 15 seconds.**

And, before you come back, take some time to reflect on how this life relates to what you've experienced.

What are the connections between the past and the present life? **Pause for 10 seconds.**

And when you're ready, slowly start to count back from ten to one.

Slowly come back into this body, into this time, so that at one, you'll be completely alert and refreshed,

And, at one, you can realize the release of these past experiences. **Pause.**

As you come back to this life, you can start to feel the negative feelings and thoughts, the images and sensations, leaving your body.

You can start to feel a deeper sense of peace and resolution about this past experience. So coming back then, ten, nine, eight, seven, six, five, four, three, two, one.

Back, relaxed and alert, and now proceed with your reflective exercises and journaling.

Track Four: Awakening Your Soul Purpose Memories

This is the exercise that will take you back into the spirit state of consciousness, just before this life, to awaken those insights regarding your unique sense of mission in this life—your soul purpose. Before you proceed with this regression exercise, take some time to review all of your reflections. What have you discovered or realized so far? This integrated imagery exercise will take you back to the before–life state. And as the laws of karma and the Cayce readings indicate, the karmic patterns or complexes and that unique sense of purpose that you carry into this life have been decided by you—and you alone.

You may get help and direction from spirit guides, but the final decisions as to the lessons and the mission in this life have been up to you. These decisions were made just prior to entering this life.

So once again, find a relaxing place to recline where you won't be disturbed, and start by focusing on the breath, taking in that sense of relaxation and trance once again and letting go of any tension or holding. And when you're ready, start to scan the body and be aware of any places of tension or holding, and through the breath, release that tension and start to relax.

Now, focus on your feet and calves and thighs and be aware of any tension or holding, and just let it go, through the breath.

Now, focus on your lower back and spinal column and shoulders. Be aware of any tension or holding, and just let it go, through the breath.

Now, focus on your abdomen and chest and throat. Be aware of any tension or holding, and just let it go, through the breath.

Now, focus on your neck and lower jaw and facial area. Be aware of any tension or holding, and just let it go, through the breath.

Now, again, you can be more and more relaxed as move you

into that deeper state of awareness and trance.

You may be aware of that deeper state of relaxation coming over as you notice your breathing getting easier, parts of your body relaxing more and more, or your body sinking into the cushion.

So whatever you notice, just relax into that deeper state of awareness. **Pause for 15 seconds.**

And, once again, in your mind's eye, go to that safe place where you feel comfortable and protected—a place where you feel safe.

And spend whatever time you need, knowing that nothing can harm you or cause you discomfort, and just take some time to relax into that place. **Pause.**

And now, as you look around, you'll see the mist ahead of you, perhaps a dense mist. **Pause for 10 seconds.**

Now, you can start to move towards that mist, still feeling safe and protected. **Pause.**

And, as you move through the mist, you'll move back into a time before this life, one that will help you to understand the karmic patterns that you bring into this life and your sense of mission and soul purpose. **Pause.**

So, start to move toward the mist, entering into the mist at one, coming out into a different state of consciousness at twenty.

Moving into the mist then, one, two; moving through, three, four, five; feeling safe and comfortable, six, seven, eight, nine, ten, eleven, twelve, thirteen,

Approaching the end, fourteen, fifteen, sixteen, seventeen, eighteen, nineteen, twenty, coming out of the mist now into the spirit state. **Pause.**

You may experience yourself above the Earth, perhaps above the town where you were born, above the country, take some time to be aware of what you're doing and thinking, and feeling in this time before this life. **Pause.**

In this spirit state, you may be aware of the presence of other souls or guides or helpers, who are there to lend advice. **Pause.**

You may be aware of memories of past lives, perhaps positive, perhaps negative.

This is where you may reflect and gain insight as to those positive characteristics and talents, skills, and ways of being that you can bring into this life. **Pause.**

And, as you look down on this life that you are about to enter, you may notice your parents or other family members, other friends, acquaintances, **Pause.**

Just notice what they're doing or saying, what they're feeling. **Pause.**

Be aware of what you are envisioning this life to be.

What is your soul purpose? **Pause.** *What are you here to accomplish?* **Pause.**

What are the interests and abilities and ways of being that you will use in this life to serve your unique purpose? **Pause.**

Listen to the advice you are given. What do they say? **Pause.**

Now, just take some time to be fully aware of the guidance you are getting and the decisions you are making. **Pause for 10 seconds.**

Is there anything else you need to know? **Pause for 10 seconds.**

Just take some time to wait for an answer.

Perhaps an answer you've been expecting, perhaps one that may be a surprise to you. **Pause for at least 15 seconds.**

Just be aware of that information that you are getting, that insight that comes to you. **Pause for 15 seconds.**

And, when you are ready, you can start to come back.

Start by slowly counting back from ten to one, so that at one, you'll be completely back, alert and refreshed, bringing with you these insights.

Starting back now, ten, nine, eight, seven, six, five, four, three, two, one. Take a breath. Just come back slowly.

And now, when you're ready, just reflect on these insights and make your journal entries.

Track Five: Awakening Perinatal Memories

Now it's time to explore that perinatal period—that time spent in utero, spent between conception and birth even though we are not fully formed physical beings This is a time we can gain experience as to what's going on in the outside world. These are experiences that you can realize still have an impact, in positive and negative ways, on our current lives. It's a time where we have a direct link into what mother and father are thinking and feeling, how they are experiencing their own lives and anticipating our birth.

It's a time where their life experiences may actually be perceived as our own. What they're thinking and feeling and sensing may be taken in as our own thoughts and feelings and sensations. And, it's a time where we can get a direct experience of our siblings and other family members. Most important, it's a time when our past-life karmic patterns and that sense of soul purpose are first imprinted on our emotional and physical bodies. These can be the first inklings of the themes or complexes that will play out in this life. And, by awakening these perinatal memories, we can gain even deeper insight into the themes we carry into this life as we move toward accentuating the positive and de-energizing the negative.

So, when you're ready, take some time to find a relaxing place to recline. And, as you close your eyes, start to scan the body and be aware again of any tension or holding. Through the breath, just release that tension or holding and start to relax.

And now, focus on your feet, again, and thighs and calves and be aware of tension or holding, and just let it go, through the breath.

Now, focus on your lower back and spinal column and shoulders, and be aware of any tension or holding and just let it go, through the breath.

Now, focus on your abdomen and chest and throat, be aware of any tension or holding and just let it go, through the breath.

Now, focus on your neck and lower jaw and facial area and be aware of any tension or holding and just let it go, through the breath.

And now, you can be more and more relaxed as you move into that deeper state of awareness and trance.

And, you can be aware of that deeper state of relaxation com-

ing over you as you notice your breathing becoming easier.

Parts of your body relaxing more and more, your body sinking deeper into the cushion.

Whatever you notice, just relax into that deeper state of awareness. **Pause for at least 10 seconds.**

And now, before you go on, just take yourself again to that safe place, where you feel protected, where nothing can harm you or cause you discomfort.

Again, be aware of what's going on around you and how you feel. **Pause.**

And now, as you move around in this safe place, find a place to recline or sit down. **Pause for 10 seconds.**

And when you're ready, just close your eyes and start to go back to earlier times in this life. **Pause.**

Take yourself back to a memory in your childhood, perhaps, when you were with your family or friends or alone playing, and just take a moment to reflect on that experience and that time. **Pause for at least 10 seconds.**

Now, go back to an even earlier time, perhaps in your infant years, perhaps just after your birth.

What are you thinking and feeling now? **Pause for 10 seconds.**

What did you sense in your body? What was going on around you?

And now, take yourself back even further to that time before your birth. **Pause.**

This is a time when you were in your mother's womb.

Just be aware of everything that's going on around you. **Pause for 10 seconds.**

What do you hear? What are they feeling? **Pause.**

What is your mother thinking and feeling and saying? **Pause.**

What do you hear and sense from your father? **Pause.**

What do you hear and feel and sense from your siblings and family members or others? **Pause.**

Just take some time to be aware of what's going on around you. **Pause for at least 15 seconds.**

And now, move on to as many experiences as you can, as you need to, and notice what's happening in each of these experiences. **Pause for 10 seconds.**

What do you hear? **Pause.**

What are you thinking? **Pause.**

What do you feel and sense in the body? **Pause.**

And when you're ready, start to be aware of how these experiences and insights relate to your life since you were born. **Pause for at least 10 seconds.**

How are these experiences relating to your past-life, between-life experiences, to your before-life decisions?

Take some time now to make all the connections that you can, all the connections that you need. **Pause for 15 seconds. This** is a time when you may stop the recording to take the time you need to process the experiences.

And when you're ready, you can start to count back again slowly from ten to one. So that at one, you'll be completely back in this time and in this body, alert and refreshed. Coming back then, ten, nine, eight, seven, six, five, four, three, two, one. Back, alert, and refreshed.

Now just take some time again to reflect on this experience and make your journal entries.

Appendix C

Frequently Asked Questions

1. **Question:** Do I have to believe in reincarnation and karma for this self-discovery approach—Integrated Imagery—to work?

   Answer: Absolutely not. Through the years I have worked with many clients who were skeptical or had no belief in reincarnation. The exercises in Sections Three and Four can work regardless of your beliefs or certainty in the principles of reincarnation. What is important is to accept the idea that your unconscious mind will reveal stories and insights that are relevant and have healing potential.

2. **Q.:** Are these past–life, between–life, before–life, and perinatal memories and experiences true or just my imagination?

   A.: For one, it really doesn't matter whether the stories are actual past–life memories or not. The stories and insights will be relevant to your current life, and they will consequently have been helpful to reflect upon. Also, it would be difficult for any of us to make up stories that are not in some way influenced by what is going on in our current life experience.

3. **Q.:** I've thought a lot about my current life through the years—and in psychotherapy—so is it necessary to spend time revisiting these insights in Section Three?

   A.: Regardless of how introspective you've been regarding your current life, these exercises will invariably provide deeper insight as to the predominant and relevant positive and negative themes in your life. Trust that there is always something to learn through this introspective self-reflective process.

4. **Q.:** I don't seem to get past–life memories or experiences in the Integrated Imagery exercises. Is that OK?

   A.: It's not always necessary to regress to past-life stories to benefit from this regression process. Again, trust that your unconscious mind is revealing insights that are relevant and can provide awareness.

5. **Q.:** I have trouble concentrating and dealing with distractions. My mind wonders off and doesn't allow me to get clear images, stories, or insights. What's wrong?

   A.: Nothing is wrong. It is not unusual, especially in the beginning, to have some difficulty concentrating and getting clear impressions. Just keep practicing and trust that the more you do, the easier the reflective regression exercises will become.

6. **Q.:** I don't get clear images of past-life stories, only thoughts and feelings. Is this working and does that matter?

   A.: No, it does not. We each process and recall memories and prior experiences differently. It's not necessary to get actual images of these past experiences. Just pay attention to the thoughts, sensations, and especially the feelings that come up.

7. **Q.:** I have problems accessing the feelings that should be associated with the memories that come up. Is that OK?

 A.: The feelings in each of your past experiences are very important to access. It is the feelings that energize these past experiences and bind these incidents, reactions, images, sensations, and scripts together. But it is not unusual that feelings—especially the difficult ones—might be difficult to access. Relax, be persistent, and trust that you will eventually be able to access what you need.

8. **Q.:** My positive complexes and experiences have been difficult to uncover. What is the problem? Does that mean that I have no positive complexes?

 A.: No, we all have a number of positive complexes, some of which will be vehicles for our unique sense of soul purpose. It is not unusual that the roots and aspects of our positive complexes are more difficult to uncover. Again, be patient and persistent. They will come to you.

9. **Q.:** I think I have a pretty good idea of the activities and ways of being that make me happy, that constitute my soul purpose. Do I have to spend time focusing on soul purpose in these exercises?

 A.: There is always something to learn regarding this critical aspect of your life. This awakening process is bound to provide new insights and/or validate more strongly what you already know about your path in this life.

10. **Q.:** Is it always necessary to redo or rescript the negative or traumatic experiences that come up?

 A.: Revisiting the traumatic past-life experiences and finishing the unfinished business is a most important way to release the negative energy of those memories. But, it's not always necessary to rehash or redo every experience. What is important is to realize the connection between those experiences of the past and to use that realization to separate the past from the present.

11. **Q.:** Is this a process that will have an immediate positive impact on my life?

    A.: Although it is possible to get immediate relief and a positive result from the exercises in this book, consider that this process of awakening is a lifelong process of self-discovery. Don't be discouraged if you don't get immediate results that transform your life overnight. Continue with the exercises and expect that you will continue to get insights which will have a cumulative impact on your well-being. You can benefit from these exercises for the rest of this life.

12. **Q.:** It's been really difficult and confusing trying to figure out how my positive and negative complexes relate to each other and interact with each other. Am I doing something wrong?

    A.: No. This is not an unusual experience. Don't get too caught up in trying to figure out all of the dynamics, interactions, and aspects of each complex. Relax and trust your unconscious mind to do the work. Just remain present and focus on the feelings and insights that come to you.

13. **Q.:** I seem to have so many different themes and complexes. It's confusing. Is this possible?

    A.: It's not unusual to have a long list of ideas, themes, and behaviors that seem to be different complexes. Start to think about how all of these seemingly different parts may actually be different aspects of just a few primary themes.

14. **Q.:** I seem to have many talents, skills, interests, and ways of being that are a part of my life. Are all of these complexes?

A.: What distinguishes a complex from a learned behavior, skill, or attitude is the level of emotional energy as well as how prominent these themes are in your life. Continue to do the Integrated Imagery and Active Imagination exercises and expect that the answer and clarity will come in time.

15. **Q.:** While doing the Integrated Imagery exercises in Section Four, I had some negative feelings and reactions that lasted for a while. What should I do?

A.: Be sure to finish the exercises by redoing those experiences to finish and de-energize those negative experiences. Finish each regression by going to your safe place before opening your eyes and coming back to the present time. If uncomfortable feelings, anxiety, or depression last for more than a day and the relaxation exercises don't seem to be giving you much relief, then that may be the time to sit down with a qualified psychotherapist to talk over and process what you've discovered.

In the course of your own process of awakening past lives, should you come up with any questions of your own or if you are interested in finding a qualified Integrated Imagery therapist, please feel free to contact me through my Web site: www.jzamoroso.com

Bibliography

Past Life Regression:

Amoroso, John Z. *Integrated Imagery: A Transpersonal Psychotherapeutic Approach*. PhD diss., The Union Institute and University, 1992.

Bolduc, Henry. *The Journey Within*. Virginia Beach, VA: Inner Vision Publishing Co., 1988.

Fiore, Edith. *The Unquiet Dead*. New York: Ballantine Books, 1987.

———. *You Have Been Here Before*. New York: Coward, McGann & Geoghegan, Inc., 1978.

Moody, Raymond. *Coming Back*. With Paul Perry. New York: Bantam Books, 1990.

———. *Life after Life*. New York: Bantam Books, 1975.

Moore, Marcia. *Hypersentience*. New York: Bantam Books, 1976.

Netherton, Morris and Nancy Shiffrin. *Past Lives Therapy*. New York: Morrow and Co., Inc., 1978.

Newton, Michael. *Journey of Souls*. St. Paul, MN: Llewellyn Publications, 2006.

———. *Life Between Lives*. St. Paul, MN: Llewellyn Publications, 2005.

Schlotterbeck, Karl. *Living Your Past Lives: The Psychology of Past-Life Regression*. New York: Ballantine Books, 1987.

Talbot, Michael. *Your Past Lives*. New York: Fawcett Crest, 1987.

Wambach, Helen. *Life Before Life*. New York: Bantam Books, 1979.

———. *Reliving Past Lives*. New York: Harper and Row, 1978.

Weiss, Brian. *Many Lives, Many Masters*. New York: Simon and Schuster, Inc., 1988.

———. *Meditation: Achieving Inner Peace and Tranquility in Your Life.* Carlsbad, CA: Hay House, Inc., 2002.

———. *Messages from the Masters.* New York: Warner Books, 2000.

———. *Mirrors of Time.* Carlsbad, CA: Hay House, Inc., 2002.

———. *Only Love Is Real.* New York: Warner Books, 1996.

———. *Same Soul, Many Bodies.* New York: Free Press, Simon & Schuster, Inc., 2004.

———. *Through Time into Healing.* New York: Simon & Schuster, Inc., 1993.

Woolger, Roger. *Healing Your Past Lives.* Louisville, CO: Sounds True, 2004.

———. *Other Lives, Other Selves.* New York: Doubleday, 1987.

Reincarnation:
Bernstein, Morey. *The Search for Bridey Murphy.* New York: Doubleday and Co., 1956.

Cerminara, Gina. *Many Lives, Many Loves.* Camarillo, CA: DeVorss & Company, 1981.

———. *Many Mansions.* New York: William Sloane, 1950.

Christie–Murray, David. *Reincarnation Ancient Beliefs and Modern Evidence.* London: Prism Press, 1988.

Cranston, Sylvia and Carey Williams. *Reincarnation: A New Horizon in Science, Religion and Society.* New York: Julian Press, 1984.

Head, Joseph and S. L. Cranston. *Reincarnation.* New York: Causeway Books, 1967.

———. *Reincarnation: The Phoenix Fire Mystery.* New York: Julian Press, 1977.

Kelsey, Denys and Joan Grant. *Many Lifetimes.* New York: Doubleday and Co., 1967.

Rogo, Scott. *The Search for Yesterday: A Critical Examination of the Evidence for Reincarnation.* Upper Saddle River, N.J.: Prentice Hall, 1985.

Sparrow, Lynn. *Reincarnation: Claiming Your Past, Creating Your Future.* New York: St. Martin's Paperbacks, 1995.

TenDam, Hans. *Exploring Reincarnation.* London: Arkana Press, 1987.

Edgar Cayce:
Bro, Harmon. *Edgar Cayce on Religion and Psychic Experience.* New York: Warner Books, Inc., 1988.

———. *A Seer Out Of Season.* New York: NAL Books, 1985.

Puryear, Herbert. *The Edgar Cayce Primer.* New York: Bantam, 1982.

Sugrue, Thomas. *There Is a River.* New York: Holt, Rinehart and Winston, 1942.

Thurston, Mark. *Discovering Your Soul's Purpose.* Virginia Beach, VA: A.R.E. Press, 1984.

———. *The Essential Edgar Cayce.* New York: Tarcher/Penguin, 2004.

———. *Paradox of Power.* Virginia Beach, VA: A.R.E. Press, 1987.

———. *Soul Purpose: Discovering and Fulfilling Your Destiny.* New York: St. Martin's Press, 1989.

———. *Synchronicity as Spiritual Guidance.* Virginia Beach, VA: A.R.E. Press, 1997.

Other Readings:
Jacobi, Jolande. *The Psychology of C. G. Jung.* New Haven: Yale University Press, 1973.

Johnson, Robert A. *Inner Work: Using Dreams and Active Imagination for Personal Growth.* New York: HarperCollins Publishing, 1986.

Jung, Carl. *Collected Works of C. G. Jung, Volume 8*. Princeton, NJ: Princeton University Press, 1969.

Maslow, Abraham. *Toward a Psychology of Being*. New York: Van Nostrand Reinhold Co., 1968.

Wade, Jenny. *Changes of Mind: A Holonomic Theory of the Evolution of Consciousness*. New York: State University of New York Press, 1996.

About the Author

John Z. Amoroso, PhD is a psychotherapist and educator located in the Philadelphia area. For more than twenty-five years he has been practicing psychotherapy utilizing the technique of Integrated Imagery and past-life regression as a primary therapeutic approach.

He is a member of the faculty of Atlantic University in Virginia Beach offering certification courses in Integrated Imagery to master's degree students and qualified professionals. In addition, he has developed a degree concentration in creativity studies for artists, business professionals, and educators.

John continues to offer workshops and certification programs in Integrated Imagery in the Philadelphia area and in private venues throughout the country. You can contact John through his website at www.jzamoroso.com

EDGAR CAYCE'S A.R.E.

Who Was Edgar Cayce?
Twentieth Century Psychic and Medical Clairvoyant

Edgar Cayce (pronounced Kay-Cee, 1877-1945) has been called the "sleeping prophet," the "father of holistic medicine," and the most-documented psychic of the 20th century. For more than 40 years of his adult life, Cayce gave psychic "readings" to thousands of seekers while in an unconscious state, diagnosing illnesses and revealing lives lived in the past and prophecies yet to come. But who, exactly, was Edgar Cayce?

Cayce was born on a farm in Hopkinsville, Kentucky, in 1877, and his psychic abilities began to appear as early as his childhood. He was able to see and talk to his late grandfather's spirit, and often played with "imaginary friends" whom he said were spirits on the other side. He also displayed an uncanny ability to memorize the pages of a book simply by sleeping on it. These gifts labeled the young Cayce as strange, but all Cayce really wanted was to help others, especially children.

Later in life, Cayce would find that he had the ability to put himself into a sleep-like state by lying down on a couch, closing his eyes, and folding his hands over his stomach. In this state of relaxation and meditation, he was able to place his mind in contact with all time and space—the universal consciousness, also known as the super-conscious mind. From there, he could respond to questions as broad as, "What are the secrets of the universe?" and "What is my purpose in life?" to as specific as, "What can I do to help my arthritis?" and "How were the pyramids of Egypt built?" His responses to these questions came to be called "readings," and their insights offer practical help and advice to individuals even today.

The majority of Edgar Cayce's readings deal with holistic health and the treatment of illness. Yet, although best known for this material, the sleeping Cayce did not seem to be limited to concerns about the physical body. In fact, in their entirety, the readings discuss an astonishing 10,000 different topics. This vast array of subject matter can be narrowed down into a smaller group of topics that, when compiled together, deal with the following five categories: (1) Health-Related Information; (2) Philosophy and Reincarnation; (3) Dreams and Dream Interpretation; (4) ESP and Psychic Phenomena; and (5) Spiritual Growth, Meditation, and Prayer.

Learn more at EdgarCayce.org.

What Is A.R.E.?

Edgar Cayce founded the non-profit Association for Research and Enlightenment (A.R.E.) in 1931, to explore spirituality, holistic health, intuition, dream interpretation, psychic development, reincarnation, and ancient mysteries—all subjects that frequently came up in the more than 14,000 documented psychic readings given by Cayce.

The Mission of the A.R.E. is to help people transform their lives for the better, through research, education, and application of core concepts found in the Edgar Cayce readings and kindred materials that seek to manifest the love of God and all people and promote the purposefulness of life, the oneness of God, the spiritual nature of humankind, and the connection of body, mind, and spirit.

With an international headquarters in Virginia Beach, Va., a regional headquarters in Houston, regional representatives throughout the U.S., Edgar Cayce Centers in more than thirty countries, and individual members in more than seventy countries, the A.R.E. community is a global network of individuals.

A.R.E. conferences, international tours, camps for children and adults, regional activities, and study groups allow like-minded people to gather for educational and fellowship opportunities worldwide.

A.R.E. offers membership benefits and services that include a quarterly body-mind-spirit member magazine, *Venture Inward*, a member newsletter covering the major topics of the readings, and access to the entire set of readings in an exclusive online database.

Learn more at EdgarCayce.org.

EDGARCAYCE.ORG